MW00623323

You *Can* Make the Horse Drink Water

Motivating Yourself and Others to Do the Best Work

Amir Bhimji, MS, MBA, MA (Organizational Psychology)
AMIRIMAGE CONSULTING INC.

P.O. Box 72164
Roselle, IL 60172
Email: amirimage@aol.com
Tel: 847-534-2732

Bhimji, Amir.
    You can make the horse drink water : motivating yourself
and others to do the best work / Amir Bhimji. --Roselle, IL :
AmirImage Consulting. 2002

        p.   cm.
    ISBN 0-9720505-0-7

    1. Motovation (Psychology)   2. Leadership   3. Self-actual-
ization (Psychology)   I. Title.

BF503.B55   2002   2002108887
153.1534--dc21   0208

Contents

Acknowledgements

First and foremost I would like to thank my daughter Alisha. Despite her busy schedule as a full-time high school math teacher while she simultaneously pursues her master's degree in education technology, she found the time to serve as my sounding board when the need arose. For that, she has my eternal gratitude.

I also need to thank the participants in my training seminars. Every time our discussions digressed to internal motivation or to the self-development model, they reacted positively. That reaction was the seed that ultimately resulted in this book. Without their interest and encouragement, it never would have materialized.

1

That "Something Within"

In September 1989 I worked as a project engineering manager and simultaneously taught a class in the District 211 adult education program. The class was titled "Holistic Self-Development." My focus in the program was on self-improvement by setting goals and becoming goal-oriented. The discussion in the third or fourth class turned to the challenges of staying focused on goals when so much unanticipated stuff happens in our lives. In that class I had a woman share a story that has stayed with me.

About three years prior to coming into my class, she shared that she was about eighty pounds overweight, smoked a lot, and had other ailments including high blood pressure and high cholesterol. Her family doctor had warned her that she was in a high-risk category for a heart attack and had urged her very strongly to make major lifestyle changes. She had tried many times to set goals, but in vain.

Then this mother of two had another child, a baby girl. Unfortunately, she soon learned that her new baby suffered a neurological condition and would be unable to take care of herself all her life. Once the gravity of this news settled in and she got past the denial stage, this woman was overcome with a determination "from within." Over the next twelve months she shed her excess weight and then some, joined a fitness class for "Moms and Tots," joined a support group, gave up smoking, took on a full-time job, and started a savings account in her daughter's name.

When I asked the woman what it was that made her so determined to turn her life around and achieve the goals she had been unable to stick with until then, she replied, "I don't know; it was just something within me. I suddenly felt driven to want to do things, and I started seeing things differently than I had before."

My Learning

This woman's story struck a chord with me. After reflecting on it for a week, I re-designed the curriculum for my class. The focus in the new design was on three key requirements for becoming successful in our personal and professional lives:

1. *We need specific goals in our personal and professional lives.*
2. *We need to become driven from within (internal motivation) in our efforts to achieve our goals.*
3. *We need to develop that special perspective (also from within) of challenges we encounter so that we do not get turned off by challenges and, in fact, may become even more driven to achieve our goals.*

Teaching this class had a major impact on me. I believe I did more learning than teaching, and the revised focus worked. My students found it very helpful and the impact for me was so great that, despite having worked my way up in my field of engineering for many years, I now seriously considered making a major change. Over the following years I went back to school for my master's degree in organizational psychology and started a new career in training design and development. My focus in my speaking and training programs became helping people build the skills to succeed in whatever it is they do by tapping into that internal motivation.

It's All about Motivation: Internal Motivation

Imagine a person having a goal of losing weight. The person can be driven to lose the weight for a variety of reasons. Let's consider a few possible reasons on a continuum as we examine the level of motivation that would be generated in each reason:

Reason 1: "I need to get on a fitness program and a diet to lose weight so I can look as good as that other person."

Reason 2: "I look awful in my summer swimsuit and I must get on a fitness program and a diet to lose weight."

Reason 3: "I hate to miss out on playing with my children while they are young and energetic. I need to get with a fitness program and a diet to lose weight so I can be physically more active and involved with them."

Reason 4: "This life is a blessing and I have so much I need to accomplish and contribute to make my life meaningful. I should get on a fitness program and a diet so I can live longer and healthier and maximize what I can accomplish in my lifetime."

See the different levels of motivation that can be generated in this simple goal we can set for ourselves? In reason one the motivation is mostly external and in reason four it is mostly internal. The more motivation that comes from within, the greater the likelihood of success. The focus in this book is helping readers tap into that internal motivation.

Benefit of This Book to You

This book can benefit you in three ways:

> *1. It can help you tap into and generate internal motivation as you pursue your personal and professional goals and through that enhance the likelihood of your success.*
>
> *2. It can help you develop a perspective whereby you perceive your challenges and frustrations in a manner that at worst does not turn you off and that at best helps you embrace those challenges as opportunities for growth.*
>
> *3. You can help others motivate themselves by role-modeling and sharing how you motivate yourself.*

What is the difference between people whose lives are average in accomplishment and people who are very successful in their accomplishments? People who are successful have goals, are driven to achieve their goals, and do not easily give up when they encounter the setbacks and frustrations we all are bound to encounter. This book addresses these very points.

My Guarantee

Let me state right up front that I cannot guarantee that the knowledge and skills from this book will help make the challenges and frustrations in your personal and professional life disappear. Not at all.

What I can guarantee is that this book can help you:

1. Develop that perspective whereby you see the same challenges and frustrations differently. This perspective will come from within you. When you see the same challenges and frustrations differently, you have in effect changed your external situation. Because you see challenges differently, you will react in a manner that is more productive.
2. Tap into a stronger motivational force from within to help you pursue your goals.

Hence, while this book cannot guarantee success, this book can guarantee your *best* effort and therefore an enhanced likelihood of success.

How Does This Play Out in the Real World?

In the real world, this plays out as follows:

- *Instead of becoming upset and angry with your boss because he does not give you the respect you deserve or because he treats you as if you are not smart, you will ask the question, "How do I build the skills I need so I do not allow this man's lack of consideration towards me to turn me off and affect my performance and growth?"*

- *As a leader in your organization, instead of becoming frustrated by constant challenges to your leadership, you will ask yourself the question, "How do I develop my self-confidence whereby I become that visionary and confident leader I admire so my people become inspired to follow my leadership?"*

- *If you find yourself in relationships where you are not treated with respect, are taken for granted, and feel insulted, you will ask yourself, "How do I enhance my self-esteem so I don't feel the need to be in relationships that are not good for me? How do I build my self-confidence so I can work on changing relationships without the fear of losing them? How do I become self-confident enough to walk*

away from relationships that I am unable to change, to walk away
from relationships that are not good for me?"

• As a parent, instead of becoming upset because your child does not
heed your well-intentioned advice to study hard and avoid keeping
bad company, you will ask yourself the question, "How do I become
the kind of parent my child will be proud of so he will consider me a
friend and trust me and heed my advice?"

• As a teacher, instead of becoming upset at the parents who do not
provide love, discipline, and support at home and instead send forth
a child who brings challenging issues for you to deal with, you will ask
the question, "How do I build the skills to address the needs the child
has and help the child realize his or her potential despite the
situation at home"

• Finally, instead of getting turned off by the "saddies, baddies,
moodies, attitudies, grouchies," and others like them in the work
place, you will ask the question, "What skills do I need to build so
I don't allow this negativity to victimize me and affect my self-
development?"

Getting the Most Out of This Book

I hope that you find this book as enjoyable to read as it was to
write. You will find that it essentially has two halves. The first half
of the book focuses on generating internal motivation and
becoming engaged in the process of continuous self-development. The second half of the book focuses on applying the self-
development model to improve your performance in your role as
an employee, manager, teacher, leader, and in your personal life.
The core of this book is on self-development. There is no way to
engage in self-development without reflection and self-analysis. I
love the comments made by Nelson Mandela on the Oprah

Winfrey show. During his interview Mr. Mandela commented that even as bad as his imprisonment of twenty-seven years was, there was an immense value in the confinement: It generated time for Mr. Mandela to reflect on his "self" and to create the change within him to become the person he was when he left the prison.

We all need periodic time for that kind of reflection and change. I strongly encourage readers to use this book as an opportunity for beginning that reflection and self-analysis.

No matter how much you might enjoy reading this book, to get the maximum value out of it I recommend that you work on the exercises contained within the chapters as well as the action plans at the end of the chapters. The objective of the exercises and the action plans is to give you specific things to work on for self-improvement. My personal experience has been that without an investment of effort to identify specific things to reflect on or specific behaviors to alter, nothing changes and no improvement takes place.

In addition, you might want to keep a journal to record your thoughts and feelings as you read this book and respond to the exercises.

The First Step in Your Journey

How do we tap into that "something within" to motivate ourselves to achieve our goals like the woman in my class? How do we shape our perspective so we can see our work as a meaningful part of our lives? How do we change our perspective so we actually welcome challenges as opportunities to grow?

The first step is to identify and enhance our awareness of the challenges we face in our personal and professional lives at this moment. That is the objective in the action plan waiting for you at the end of this chapter.

The next step is to understand in a systematic fashion what is that "something within" from which we get our perspective and our internal motivation. That is the focus in the next chapter, "Computer Program, Human Program."

Action Plan

1. *Identify three specific challenges or problems you face in your workplace that you would love to change. What are the specific issues? With whom do you have them? What impact do these challenges have on your performance?*

2. *Identify three specific challenges or problems you face in your personal life. What are the specific issues? With whom do you have them? What impact do these challenges have on you?*

2

Computer Program, Human Program

An analogy I like to use to illustrate how our perspective of our world is shaped involves the computer. Take the computer you have at home as an example. Whether it is a PC or a Mac, your computer is programmed and the output of your computer is a function of that "program."

Similarly, our personal output or performance is a function of our program. This internal human program distinguishes two human beings, because no two individuals will react the same to any external situation. While one becomes stressed out and has an anxiety attack, the other takes it in stride. What generates this different reaction or performance is the internal human program. Different terms are used to refer to this internal program, the more common ones being "self-image" and "self-concept," defined as how we see our overall selves.

Let us continue the analogy of our internal program, our "self-image," to a computer program:

- *The computer's program determines the computer's output; our personal performance in life is determined by our self-image.*
- *Someone somewhere decided how our computers were going to be programmed. In other words, it was done by design. The computer's programming did not just happen on its own.*

In your case, did you even play a role in how you were pro-grammed? The term we use to characterize the process by which human beings are programmed is "by default." In other words, our programming just happens starting from the day we are born and is based in great part on the messages we receive. These mes-sages might be anything from, "There is absolutely nothing you cannot achieve or become if you set your mind to it" to "College is just not for you and you might as well forget it."

- *If we are unhappy with our computer's performance, we have choices such as taking it to a computer store for service and/or an upgrade or buying a new computer.*

If we are unhappy with our internal program or self-image and have feelings such as, "Why do I allow him to drive me up the wall?" or "I hate this thing about myself," there is, unhappily, no "self-image store." The good news is that you and I can change our internal program ourselves, once we understand the compo-nents, the linkage, and the process.

- *When we want to improve the performance of our computer, we might use the terms "re-programming" or "upgrading." When we want to improve our personal performance through improvement in our self-image, the term we use is "self-development."*

- *Can we ever have a most up-to-date computer that stays up-to-date forever? We really cannot, considering the speed with which computer technology is moving ahead. It requires a constant effort at re-programming or upgrading to stay up-to-date. Similarly, self-development is a life-long process that involves continuous improvement of our self-image.*

- *A virus in the computer is something that can negatively impact its performance and is something that should be addressed. Similarly,* we can have inadequacies or complexes in our self-image that can negatively impact our performance and they, too, need to be addressed.

• When you think about your computer at home, what makes up the components of its program? In lay terms, these include its operating system, software, processor, speed, memory, etc.

What makes up the components of our internal program or self-image? The components are things such as the following:

1.   What is your personal vision for your life? What do you think about life itself? What do you feel is your "sense of purpose"? This is where you and I get our sense of direction, our drive to pursue goals, and our resolve to not give up when we run into roadblocks.

2.   What is your value system? This is where we get our priorities and clarity of what is important to us, and from this comes the quality of "decisiveness," the ability to make decisions without undue procrastination.

3.   What is your belief system? This includes and goes beyond religious beliefs to what we believe about life, ourselves, and others. For example, you may believe people are lazy and not to be trusted, that life is just a chance event and there is no accountability beyond this life, that abortion is a sin, and so on.

4.   What are your perceptions about your "self"? This includes perceptions of your physical self, mental self, physiological self, social self, emotional self, spiritual self, sexual self, etc. What specific things about yourself seem like inadequacies to you? Our perceptions determine how we feel about ourselves: good or embarrassed or something in between. This influences the complexes we develop when interacting with others and the outcomes from those interactions.

5.   What are your perceptions about your abilities and accomplishments? This is where we might think to ourselves, "I wish I could talk

like that" or "I wish I had those social skills." The focus here is on the inventory of skills built to date and our perceptions about them.

6. What are your perceptions about your potential? What do you believe about how far and how high you can or cannot go? Some of the thoughts here might be, "There is nothing I cannot do if I really want to" or "I could never handle the responsibilities of a leader."

7. What are your perceptions about "others?" This influences how we treat and behave with others and the resulting quality of our relationships with them.

8. What are your expectations about "self" and "others"? This influences the sense of frustration and stress we experience when things don't measure up to our expectations, as well as the delight we feel when they exceed our expectations.

Improvement in the Computer Programming

If we were to represent the re-programming or upgrading of our computers with an illustrative model, it would be a simple model with two steps. Step "A" would represent the existing computer, and Step "B" would represent the new, improved computer. The movement from Step "A" to Step "B" we would call "upgrading" or "re-programming." This schematic illustration of our re-programming/upgrading is shown in Figure 1 below:

Figure 1

Improvement in Our Internal Program or Self-Image

If we were to work on improving our self-image instead of our computer programs, a similar model as above would represent the improvement process. Instead of "re-programming" or "upgrading," we would be engaged in the process of "self-development." This is represented in Figure 2:

Figure 2

Examples of Self-Development

Let me choose a simple example to discuss an improvement in my self-image. Let's say in one of the components of my self-image, my physical self, I am unhappy with my nose. It is too big and too bulbous and I am always conscious of it, always comparing it with others. I have wished for years that I had a smaller, thinner, and cuter nose. After years of agonizing and reflection, I have decided this is important to me and that I want to spend the money to undergo cosmetic surgery. This I do.

Let's say that two weeks after the cosmetic surgery, when the bandages have been removed and the scars have healed, I look at the nose and feel good about my appearance. I feel better about my new physical self and hence better about my self-image. This is one example of "self-improvement" or "self-development."

Now let us look at another example of self-development.

While I was still in engineering, I suddenly became aware that most of my engineer friends were getting their MBA (master's in business administration) degrees. To be honest, I felt an inferiority complex that I did not belong to that club of engineers with MBAs. After some agonizing, I decided to go to night school even as I worked a full-time job. After a period of three years, I earned my MBA. This is another example of self-development. Getting the MBA enhanced my perception of my "mental self," a component of my self-image.

Years later, while working in an organization and while I was still in engineering, I had an opportunity to do some technical training for employees on the third shift. I liked the aspects of training so much that I mentioned to my manager that I would love to do this work full-time. My manager was very accommodating and put me in touch with the training department and gave me a very good recommendation. I was informed that there was no current opening in the training department and I had to remain in engineering for the time being. I realized that most trainers had some background in organization development, or education, and so to improve my credentials I considered going to school for my master's in organizational psychology. Once again, even though I was still in engineering, my manager found a way for me to go to school and qualify for re-imbursement.

No sooner did I earn the degree than I made the move into training full-time, and I have been doing it ever since. This is yet another example of self-development. I was now in a field I loved more and I had earned the credentials to feel competent as a trainer. This career change enhanced my perception of my "abilities, accomplishments, and potential," another component in my self-image.

Examples of Self-Development for You

The examples cited in the preceding section illustrate the change we are talking about as part of our continuous self-development. The change can be an improvement in any one or more components of our self-image. It can be in our physical self, mental self, spiritual self, abilities and accomplishments, vision, value system, belief system, perceptions of others, or in our expectations.

I shared with you examples of what constituted self-development for me. Now think about your present situation and what changes would constitute self-development for you. Also, under what component of self-image would these changes belong?

Why You Should Commit to Continuous Self-Development

I want to make a case for why you should commit to continuous self-development. If I do a good job, then hopefully you will never look back without finding yourself engaged in self-development.

You can improve a computer all you want. You might feel very good about it, but your computer has no emotions, either of sadness or happiness. However, human beings do have emotions and feelings. Let's take a look at what happens when I improve my self-image in several different components.

Let's say that over the course of three years I make the following improvements:

1. *I have undergone plastic surgery for improvement in my nose.*

2. *I have gone back to school and received my master's degree in psychology.*
3. *I have enrolled at a gym and have built a very good, muscular body.*
4. *I have been reading books on spirituality and have gained immense clarity about my spiritual self.*
5. *I have developed a great and meaningful relationship with the bright woman I met at the bookstore.*
6. *I have been awarded a patent for my work and consequently have received a major promotion.*

As a result of these changes, I feel better about my overall self. This generation of good feelings about my self is called "self-esteem." I have yet to meet a person who does not relish having high self-esteem. What better reason can I give you to get engaged in continuous self-development? Having high self-esteem helps us in the work place and in our personal relationships. People like to be around people with high self-esteem. Those with high self-esteem perform better in teams at work. Schematically, the incorporation of self-esteem into our self-development model is illustrated in Figure 3:

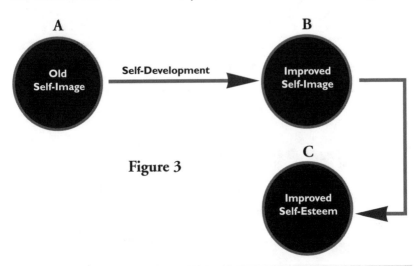

Figure 3

Action Plan

When you are ready for reflecting on your own self-image, here is what is waiting for you: Appendices A, B, and C.

Appendix A: Establishing a Baseline for Your Present Self-Image

The main objective here is to help you think through the various components of your self-image and to identify the hang-ups and inadequacies that might exist for you.

Appendix B: The Process of Continuous Self-Development

This section will illustrate a process of self-development to address those inadequacies and in the process elevate your self-image.

Appendix C: Building a Strong, Healthy, and Positive Self-Image

Now that you know the process to address inadequacies, this section will help you think through and re-define each component of your self-image to create the self-image you want.

3

Self-Esteem and Self-Confidence

Take another look at Figure 3 and you will see that our self-esteem is generated from our self-image. These two concepts go hand in hand. Self-image is how we see our overall self and self-esteem is defined as a "measure" or "value" we place on our self-image.

Hence, a poor self-image corresponds with low self-esteem. A strong, healthy, and positive self-image corresponds with high self-esteem. This relationship between self-image and self-esteem is illustrated in Figure 4:

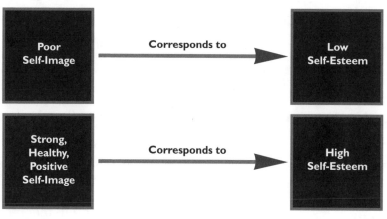

Figure 4

Internal Source of Self-Esteem

This source of our self-esteem that is generated from our self-image is "internal." The more we improve our self-image by working on the various components, such as physical self, mental self, abilities and accomplishments, and so on, the higher our self-esteem. This self-esteem that is generated from within I call "true" or "genuine" or "real" or "internal" self-esteem. This is to differentiate it from another source of self-esteem we call "apparent" or "external" self-esteem.

External Source of Self-Esteem

Let me ask you a question I ask participants in my class called "Self-Awareness for Self-Growth": How would you feel if your manager walked up to you and said, "I want you working on this new team and then, when you walked into the first meeting of this new team, the very first person you ran into said, "Are you working on this team? That is great! I think it is going to be a fun experience working with you. I am excited. Here, have a seat."

Would this greeting boost or enhance your self-esteem? (Most participants generally respond with a smile and say, "Yes, it would boost my self-esteem.")

Now let's change the outcome of this same situation. Your manager walks up to you and asks you to go work on this new team. As you walk into the first meeting of this new team, the very first person you run into says, "Are you working on this team? What happened; they didn't want you on the other team, huh?"

Would this interaction deflate your self-esteem? (Most

participants generally respond without a smile and say, "Yes, it would deflate my self-esteem.")

Then I make the point that this is not true self-esteem. True self-esteem comes from within. This is "apparent" or "external" self-esteem and is self-esteem created by others. We all have worked with people who like us, admire us, and praise us and we do feel better about ourselves. On the other hand, when we work with people who are critical of us and believe that we are not smart, we come away feeling poorly about ourselves.

Examples of External Sources of Self-Esteem

When participants in my classes say to me that "I had such high self-esteem until I started working for that woman, and then the way she treated me I lost it all" or with regards to relationships, "I had such high self-esteem until I got into a relationship with this guy, and then the way he treated me, I lost my self-esteem," my response is, "I hate to say it, but unfortunately you really didn't have it; if others 'giveth,' then others can 'taketh'."

Think about and identify situations where you experience a boost to your self-esteem from external sources. If you are in relationships where others put you on a pedestal and it enhances your self-esteem, that is an external source of self-esteem. In my case, when I do a talk and feel good about my style, my content, and having achieved my outcome, that is internal self-esteem. If I hang around after the talk just to receive positive comments from the participants and feel good based on those comments, that is external self-esteem.

Internal Versus External Self-Esteem

Which one is better, self-esteem that is generated from within or self-esteem generated externally? Both are good, yet no one can take away the self-esteem that is generated internally. Self-esteem has two components, internal and external. The stronger the internal component, the less you are at the mercy of the external component.

This is not to imply that self-esteem generated from external sources is bad. It is to imply that self-esteem solely generated from external sources is risky. It can make or break your day. Ideally, we all would love to live and work in a world where everyone around us is always letting us know, "You are the greatest; you are the best."

Unfortunately, this is not the real world. Hence, we must build our internal self-esteem the best we can and keep enhancing it continuously.

Deficiency in Self-Esteem

A deficiency in self-esteem can arise for a variety of reasons. A child brought up from infancy with no positive messages and only negative messages about his or her abilities and intelligence will invariably grow up with a lack of self-esteem. This lack of self-esteem will play out in the child's behaviors in the classroom and on the playground. Using the computer analogy, all children are born with a clean hard drive in their program or self-image. The parents are the first master programmers to write on the clean hard drive.

The first opportunity to compensate for the lack of self-esteem derived at home comes when the child starts going to school. Here, the behaviors of a child with low self-esteem might include not participating in class for fear of saying the wrong thing, not doing homework, a lack of interests, not being assertive in interactions with other children, easily giving up play equipment to others, and so on. Depending on how the teacher reacts to these behaviors, the low self-esteem can be reinforced. With the best of intentions, the teacher might make comments like, "See how Lisa is answering questions? You too should raise your hand like Lisa when I ask a question." The child with low self-esteem who hears this will feel an inadequacy of not measuring up to Lisa and his or her low self-esteem will be reinforced.

However, if the teacher is able to look beyond the behaviors, the teacher can shape the teacher-child interactions to boost the self-esteem of the child. This might be done with comments such as, "I have no doubt that you can do this work once you learn how and I can help you learn" or "I have total confidence that you are very smart on the inside; you have just not learned how to do it yet and I can help you" or "I am convinced that you are just as smart as anyone else and don't you let anyone tell you that you are not." In effect, the teacher can re-write the program in the self-image or, better yet, install an anti-virus program to protect the child against future viruses.

If this child grows up with no major intervention to correct the low self-esteem started at home, his or her poor perception of "self" can become engrained to the point where the young man or woman now actually believes that he or she is not as smart as the others and develops an "inferiority complex."

Low self-esteem can also play out in behaviors different than just withdrawal and non-participation. It can play out in submissive behaviors where the person compensates for low self-esteem by trying to appease others or by sacrificing his or her own interests to accommodate the interests of others. Others might compensate for low internal self-esteem by presenting an image on the outside that appears to reflect a very high self-esteem. This artificially inflated self-esteem or superiority complex is illustrated best in the behaviors displayed by Archie Bunker in the *All in the Family* television sitcom of many years ago. The tendency here is to compensate for the deficiency in internal self-esteem by looking down on others, finding a flaw in others, to artificially make the "self" look and feel better.

Self-Esteem Scale

All human beings like to have high self-esteem. We might not consciously think about it, but we all like to feel good about ourselves. I know of no human being who wakes up in the morning and goes to work with the feeling that "Today if I am treated badly and made to feel poorly about myself, it's okay." So in this chapter I want to focus on what we can do to move our self-esteem higher and higher.

Imagine that we have a scale of self-esteem from a low of "1" to a high of "10" as illustrated below. A question you want to ask yourself periodically is, "Where am I on this scale of '1' to '10?'" and "What can I do to take it higher?"

1 | | | | | | | | | | 10

Low Self-Esteem   **High Self-Esteem**

Self Esteem Scale

What Does a "1" on the Self-Esteem Scale Look Like?

A "1" on the self-esteem scale indicates low self-esteem. What does low self-esteem look like? Let us first look at self-esteem that is generated from within. Low self-esteem would mean that the person has a poor self-image of himself or herself. The person feels extremely poorly about many of the components in his or her self-image. As an example, the person might believe the following:

- *My physical appearance is embarrassing.*
- *Mentally I am not as astute as others.*
- *Life has no meaning at all and there is no purpose to it.*
- *People cannot be trusted and I have to watch them; otherwise they will take advantage of me.*

Now let's imagine how a person with true low self-esteem might handle compliments from others. Since the person does not think much of himself or herself, the person cannot accept genuine comments of praise from others because these comments conflict with what the person believes about himself or herself. Self-esteem is thus not enhanced from either external sources or internal sources and the person remains low on the scale.

What Does a "10" on the Self-Esteem Scale Look Like?

A person with high self-esteem feels self-assured. His or her self-esteem is generated from within. As an example, a person high on the scale of self-esteem might believe the following:

- *I feel good about my physical appearance. I wish I had more hair, but I can live with what I have.*

- *I feel good about my ability to learn.*
- *There is a purpose to life and I must stay focused on it.*
- *Some people might have gone bad, but most are good like me and can be fun.*

A person with high self-esteem accepts comments of praise with appreciation to the people doing the complimenting. This person can also accept constructive feedback with ease. Having high self-esteem that is generated from within, this person is not easily threatened and made insecure.

Importance of Self-Esteem in Our Interactions

The true test of a person's self-esteem is determined in challenging situations. Let's consider a situation where a man has had a bad day at work and feels miserable about the way he was treated. He walked into his workplace in the morning with a smile on his face and with the intention of wanting to make it a good day. He greeted the first person he ran into with a smile and a warm "Good morning." Instead of a gracious response, he got the curt response, "What's so good about it? Keep your 'Good mornings' to yourself." Later in the morning he failed a simple test to qualify for working in the sales department. He heard others laughing at his responses in the test, and he feels he is not good at anything.

He returned home at the end of the day feeling awful and opened the front door of his house. As he entered his home his little daughter ran towards him with tears in her eyes. Sobbing, she said to her father, "Daddy, I don't want to go to school tomorrow. They called me 'stupid' and they won't play with me. Please, Daddy, don't make me go to school tomorrow."

In this instant the father has to enhance his little daughter's self-esteem about herself, but he cannot do it very well if his own self-esteem is low.

Interactions play out similarly in the workplace and in personal relationships. Let's consider a manager who has to give feedback on some sensitive issues to an employee. To enhance the likelihood that the feedback will be received the way it should be, the challenge for the manager is to deliver the feedback in a manner that maintains or enhances the employee's self-esteem. The manager cannot do a good job of giving feedback and meeting that criteria if his or her self-esteem is not very high.

Consider another example I have witnessed in many organizations. Imagine that a worker is not wearing safety glasses and earplugs in a factory environment where such protective equipment is required. Some of the many ways I have witnessed this behavior addressed include the following:

- *If you have a death wish go elsewhere, but here you must wear that safety stuff.*

- *Make this your last time, but don't let me catch you again without your earplugs.*

- *You should know better. This safety requirement is for your own good, so why don't you wear it?*

- *Go ahead and dare me if you want to. If I see you tomorrow without your safety equipment, you will be history.*

- *Listen, you need your vision and hearing for your family. You don't want to miss out on the sights and sounds. So please put on the eye glasses and earplugs right now. Thanks. Now I feel better.*

Imagine you are a manager walking through the manufacturing area and you see one of the workers lifting a fifty-pound bag improperly. (The correct way to lift it is by bending the knees.) Think about what you would say to correct the worker's behavior. The best one I heard in my many plant tours was this: "You know, we will be lost without you if you come down with a disc problem in your back. Bend those knees, will you? Thanks."

In fact, I state in my seminars that there is nothing you cannot say to someone as long as you say it in a manner that maintains or preferably enhances the other person's self-esteem. This is a good criteria to use for every interaction we have.

Enhancing the External Component of Self-Esteem

We have defined self-esteem as having two components, one internal and one external. Let's focus first on what kinds of things we might be able to do to enhance our self-esteem through optimizing the external component. Here are some items that can help:

- *Surround yourself with people who care about you and can be supportive of you.*
- *Pre-empt negative comments from those you feel have a negative perception of you. You can pre-empt them by building them into the expectations in your mindset so that you are not shocked or turned off when you hear them.*
- *Seek feedback from those who care about you on how you can handle the negative comments that might come your way.*
- *Develop a support system of people you trust whom you can turn to when you need a boost in your self-esteem.*
- *Build your skills so you react assertively to comments and actions from*

others that are intended to lower your self-worth.

- *Do some self-analysis regarding what buttons within you are being pushed or what sensitive spots are being rubbed the wrong way. Becoming aware is the first step in addressing these sensitivities.*

Enhancing the Internal Component of Self-Esteem

Consider the house you presently live in. Every improvement you make in the house improves it's value. Similarly, every improvement we make in our self-image improves its value, or our self-esteem. If the house is well designed in all areas but one, this one undeveloped area takes away from the value of the house. This is very much like the analogy of a wheel with spokes: The weakest spoke determines the strength of the wheel. Similarly, just like the weakest spoke, an inadequacy in the self-image can undermine the self-esteem. In that wheel you need to fix the weakest spoke to make the wheel reliable. In your self-esteem, you need to fix the inadequacy to make the self-esteem serve your needs.

Self-Confidence

Self-confidence is defined as a feeling of "I can." It is a feeling of competence in one's self. Say two people with the same educational background and same work experience are introduced to a new skill to be performed in the workplace. One is unsure of his ability to perform the new skill and the other is confident with the feeling, "If others can, I can." Guess what? The probability is greater that the self-confident person will be more successful.

A person who is engaged in the process of continuous

self-development who also has high self-esteem will display behaviors that reflect the following:

- *The person is more self-assured.*
- *The person is more willing to take risks.*
- *The person is less concerned about how he or she is perceived by others in case of failure.*
- *The person is able to acknowledge areas of weakness in his or her self and doesn't flaunt strengths in his or her self.*
- *The person can handle failure or setbacks as learning opportunities and is not unduly embarrassed by the thought of failure.*

An analysis of the behaviors just identified indicates that they also are the behaviors a self-confident person will display. This self-confidence generated in this fashion is internally generated. The relationship of these concepts is illustrated in Figure 5. Just as we found that there are two sources of self-esteem, one internal and one external, so also are there two sources of self-confidence, one internal as illustrated in Figure 5, and one external:

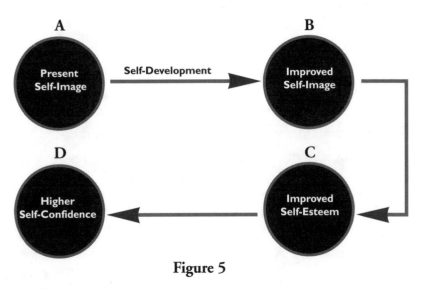

Figure 5

External Source of Self-Confidence

Recall any situation you have experienced in which another person displayed more confidence in you than you had in yourself. This might have been in school with a teacher, in sports with a coach, or in the workplace with a manager. You will typically find that the experience had a positive impact on you and that you went the extra mile or put in the extra effort needed as a result of the higher confidence the other person displayed in you.

In my case, I have been fortunate to have experienced numerous situations where others had more confidence in me than I had in myself and I was inspired to put in the extra effort so as not to disappoint the person who displayed the confidence in me. Again, I did not necessarily achieve the desired outcome in every instance, but in those instances where I did achieve the desired outcome, it boosted my self-confidence to tackle even more challenging tasks.

For instance, when I was at the young age of nine, my father encouraged me to talk within my community to groups as large as one hundred or more. He displayed confidence in me as being good at communication and he would also mention to others with pride that "My son will be giving a talk next week." After the talk, no matter how I felt about my performance, he always said, "You did good. I knew all along that you could do it. You should feel good about what you can do." For me such experiences were like magic. All apprehensions were gone and I would look for another opportunity to do another talk.

Three specific ways you can enhance self-confidence from external sources include the following:

1. Identify and take on tasks that are reachable and yet slightly challenging. Every time you accomplish a goal it enhances your self-confidence to take on even more challenging tasks.

2. Seek out managers to work for and people to work with who have high self-confidence themselves. Such people display confidence in you and boost your confidence. Managers can give you assignments that are challenging and the support and confidence to succeed, and then every experience of success boosts your self-confidence.

3. Display genuine belief and confidence in others in the studies or work they are engaged in. Become a cheerleader. Every time they succeed and express their appreciation to you for your help, it enhances your confidence. "After all, if I have the skills to help others succeed, I certainly have the skills to help myself succeed."

Self–Motivation

See what happens when we engage in the process of self-development? With improvement in the self-image comes higher self-esteem and higher self-confidence. And once we have experienced higher self-esteem and higher self-confidence, we like the "taste," we like the feeling. The natural reaction is to seek more of what we like. We do just that by re-engaging in the process of self-development. This motivation to repeat the cycle generates even higher self-esteem with motivation to repeat the cycle again. Now the process has become self-motivating, as illustrated in Figure 6 below:

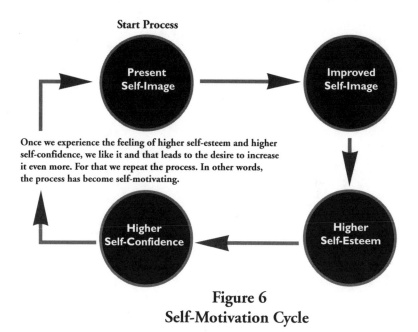

Start Process

Present Self-Image → Improved Self-Image

Once we experience the feeling of higher self-esteem and higher self-confidence, we like it and that leads to the desire to increase it even more. For that we repeat the process. In other words, the process has become self-motivating.

Higher Self-Confidence ← Higher Self-Esteem

Figure 6
Self-Motivation Cycle

Action Plan

1. *Identify two specific things you will do to enhance your self-esteem.*

2. *Identify two specific things you will do to enhance your self-confidence.*

4

Application of Self-Development Model to Performance Improvement

Why do two people in the same job situation with the same knowledge and skills perform so very differently? Because in addition to the knowledge and skills required to perform the job, our performance is tempered by factors within our self-image that influence how we perceive our work environment specifically, and the world around us generally.

Our Self-Image Shapes Our World View

Our self-image has an impact at multiple levels because of the various components comprising our self-image. In addition to generating our sense of esteem, it generates a whole host of other senses such as our sense of confidence, our sense of identity, our sense of belonging, our sense of purpose, our sense of direction, our sense of worth, etc. These senses act as filters or lenses through which we see the world and the people in the world. These filters or lenses shade our view of the world. This is illustrated in Figure 7 on following page:

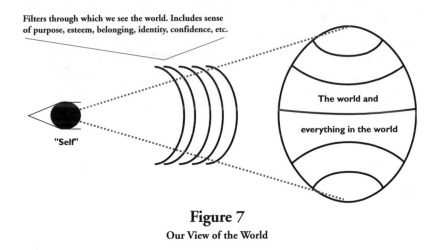

Figure 7
Our View of the World

Our World View Shaped by an Under-Developed Self-Image

Our world view influences the quality of our interactions and our performance. An under-developed self-image shapes our world view in a particular manner. Let's analyze a few examples:

- *If I as a person from India do not have a good sense of identity based on where I come from and my ethnic background, this will influence my perception of the world. I might envy others who have a sense of identity they feel good about.*

- *If Jack has a low sense of esteem, his interactions will be influenced by his low sense of esteem. This might play out in so many different ways. He might not trust and be unable to accept genuine compliments that are paid to him for his skills. Or he might compensate for his low sense of esteem by projecting an image that represents an artificially high sense of esteem that actually is perceived as a superiority complex.*

- *If Jamie has grown up with little or no sense of belonging at home, she will seek ways to stay away from home as much as possible or to stay put in her room or in her corner of the house. Imagine that Jamie encounters a group of students in her school into drugs, sex, and stealing. Jamie is not into those things, but the group offers her a sense of belonging and worth that she has never experienced before. It is very possible that Jamie might just join the group. And if the group is able to satisfy Jamie's need for belonging, she might just want to be an active part of the negative activities of the group to keep earning that sense of belonging.*

Our World View Shaped
by a Well-Developed Self-Image

A strong, healthy, positive self-image generates a whole host of improved senses that become filters through which we see the same world differently. Armed with high self-esteem and high self-confidence, we see the glass as "half full" rather than "half empty." This positive perspective of everything around us influences how we perceive people, things, and situations. As illustrated below in some sample situations, this perspective positively impacts all skill areas including leadership, coaching, managing conflict, teaching, conducting performance appraisals, giving and receiving feedback, customer service, leveraging diversity, creating inclusion, and building relationships, to name a few:

- *A manager in the workplace who believes in the employee can give feedback in a manner in which it can be received well. The self-assured manager can also receive feedback without going on the defensive.*
- *A leader who has a personal vision is in a better position to align the organizational vision with the personal vision and to display passion*

when communicating the organizational vision.

- *A teacher in the classroom who has confidence in the student who is not performing well can respond in a manner so as to inspire the student to expend extra effort on his or her studies.*
- *A supervisor who has clarity of his or her values is able to make timely decisions without undue procrastination.*
- *A clerk who has high self-esteem can provide consistently great customer service to the irate client.*
- *A self-confident person, when challenged, can maintain "cool" composure and not react at an emotional level to turn a situation into a conflict.*

Victim Mentality: The Risk of Low Self-Esteem

One of the many risks of low self-esteem in the workplace is that when we encounter negative interactions, there is a tendency to personalize them. This personalization can extend to the point of paralysis, at which any one of us can fall into the "victim mentality" mode.

"Victim Mentality" Defined

A "victim mentality" can be defined as the feeling of being a victim to perceived "unfair treatment." Whether the treatment is genuinely unfair or not does not matter for the feeling of victimization to exist. For the person who has this feeling of victimization, his or her perception is reality.

My "Victim Mentality" Experience

I had been employed all of my adult life until I became a consultant on my own. I can recall a performance review I once received in which my manager gave me a salary increase that was less than average for the group I worked in. I was expecting a higher percentage based on my manager's appraisal in an earlier mid-year review, so I was very disappointed with the salary review. I believed that my manager did not like me as much as he liked the others. How did I react to this feeling of disappointment?

I chose not to do my best work. I did what was assigned to me and no more. My thoughts were, "Why bother doing the best? If they're not going to appreciate me, I will not do any more than I need to."

The Price for "Victim Mentality"

The following mid-year review was even worse than the preceding one, and the following salary adjustment was substantially below average. I genuinely was not enjoying my work anymore and this was reflected in my performance. Now when I think about my reaction to the first lower-than-expected salary review, my thoughts are, "How dumb was I? I failed to realize that when I chose to lower my performance, I was hurting myself even more. Not only did my subsequent performance reviews get worse, my own learning and development declined during that period. I hurt myself more than any hurt caused by my manager."

Reasons for "Victim Mentality"

In the speaking and training I do, I run into many people who perceive receiving "unfair treatment" and share that they feel like "victims." Many more might not consider themselves as "victimized" but acknowledge that they are not driven to perform at any more than an "average" level. They think, "Why bother when no one appreciates the extra effort?" Some of the reasons I have heard for people feeling "victimized" include the following:

- *I deserved the promotion that went to someone else.*
- *All the company cares about is the bottom line; they don't care about people.*
- *My boss is prejudiced against me.*
- *I am given "filler" stuff; others get the "plum" assignments.*
- *They "talk the talk"; they don't "walk the talk."*
- *The people I work with don't include me in their network.*
- *They don't solicit my participation or input in the meetings.*
- *I was never made to feel part of the team; I was barely introduced to my workgroup from the time I was hired.*
- *I am excluded from their after-work social activities.*

My Current Response to "Victim Mentality": *Self-Development*

In my case, I was very fortunate that the self-development concept dawned on me. I realized that I was hurting my own learning and development and that there had to be another way to respond to challenges and negativity. I kept searching for that other way and, as luck would have it, I came upon another challenge in the workplace.

I found myself working for another manager who used extremely directive comments in his interactions with me. His comments to me sounded like orders: "I don't want to hear you bring this up in the meeting," "I need you to complete this project in three weeks," "I cannot accept that as a reason for the delay." What made the comments sound even worse was that in meetings those directive comments were aimed primarily at me. In his interactions with others his comments were much more gracious and included niceties such as, "Please," "I need your help," "Do me a favor, will you?" and so on.

This time my response was different. I was determined to build the skills so that not only could I cope with this manager, I would keep my performance from slackening. I took it as a challenge. I worked hard and did my job well. I tried very hard not to feel insulted by my manager's directive style and I stuck with my approach for over a year. My manager's style with me stayed basically the same over the period, but I noticed a slight change in the non-verbal cues. There was more smiling with me and a few more compliments with "Thank you" occasionally added. Gradually his interaction style with me became better than it used to be, though it was never quite as warm as with others.

I moved on to another opportunity a year later, but I felt good that I had not allowed one individual's negativity to affect my learning and growth. In fact, my self-confidence increased as a result of this experience. I felt confident and competent to handle even bigger challenges.

Based on my own experiences, some of which I have shared here and elsewhere in this book, I can understand how easily good people can get "turned off" in the workplace. My treatment, while certainly negative, was of a subtle nature and covert. However, if the treatment violates laws, statutes, or policies then by all means seek redress with the authorities within the organization and without. My experience from talking to people in my classes has been that most people are impacted by subtle negative behaviors in their organizations. My point in these situations is that how we respond determines our learning, growth, and development. It is in our best interests to not allow subtle negative treatment to "turn us off." This is where the self-development model can be very helpful.

Your "Victim Mentality" Experience

Take some time to reflect on and make notes in your journal about one or two situations where you experienced "victim mentality." This can be from your personal or professional life.

- *What were the specifics of the situation and your perception of the unfair treatment?*
- *Who was the source of your unfair treatment?*
- *How long did the treatment last?*
- *What was your reaction then? How do you feel about it now?*
- *What price did you pay in terms of your learning, growth, and development?*
- *What have you learned? What will you do differently now?*

We All Have It within Us

My biggest learning from my own experience was that we all have whatever it is we need to do our "best work" right within us. It is more than just changing behaviors. There is an internal component within us that needs to be tapped.

I had a neighbor, Pat, many years ago who would come to his home in the evenings very frustrated. His comments to me often were as follows: "Amir, you speak such good English; how come the people I work with can't speak like you do? It is so hard to understand them. It is so frustrating and it drives me up the wall."

This went on for almost a year. Then one day Pat just quit his job. He stayed home for a while contemplating what he wanted to do, and then the next thing I knew, Pat had bought a dry cleaning store. I lost contact with him for some time while he was establishing his business. Then one Saturday I had to go pick up some clothes from his store and I observed something I would never have thought possible.

While I waited in Pat's store, at least three or four clients came in, mostly to drop clothes off, and not one of them spoke "good" English. One of them in particular spoke no English! I saw Pat somehow figure out a way of communicating with his client with patience and with charm. At one point he pulled out a shirt on a hanger and a folded shirt to find out how the woman wanted her clothes. Pat was ingenious. His approach was very creative and it worked extremely well. It dawned on me that this was the same Pat who used to complain about problems communicating with people who did not speak very well. Pat had it within him all along.

Hence, in the chapters that follow, you will see that to become better in your work as a teacher, as a manager, or in any capacity, my focus is on behavior as well as on the internal component, or that something within us.

A Strategy to Get Engaged in Self-Development

A simple strategy to get engaged in the process of self-development is this: Anytime you perceive that you are experiencing subtle negative treatment, ask this question: "What skills do I need to build so I do not allow this negative treatment to slow my learning, growth, and development?"

Asking this question in this form can lead to answers that can do the following:

> 1. *They can keep you from falling into the "victim" mode.*
> 2. *They can get you engaged in the self-development mode.*
> 3. *They can generate answers that will help you build skills to cope with this type of negative treatment in the future.*

The "Personal Case" for Continuous Performance Improvement

I myself have felt this way and have heard many people express the feeling that "I will not be paid any more, so why perform any better?" My response is that you want to do your "best work" more for yourself than for the organization. I want to make a personal case for this point of view:

- *There are no guarantees in life but the likelihood of success is greater and the probability higher if you keep your skills and competencies developed to the maximum extent possible.*
- *To me there is no such thing as staying at a fixed level. If you are not moving forward, you are moving backward. Technology and everything else around us is advancing all the time; if we don't keep pace, we fall behind. Going back to our computer analogy, if we don't keep our computers updated and upgraded, in due course they become obsolete. So do we.*
- *Even if you are planning to make a move to another organization, it still makes sense to stay engaged in continuous self-development.*
- *The more we build our skills and competencies when we are engaged in doing our "best work," the more it enhances our self-confidence and through that our self-esteem and self-image.*

• *Studies have shown that just the process of being mentally engaged has a positive impact on our mental and physiological well-being.*

Other Strategies for Performance Improvement

Overcoming Natural Tendencies

If you sense any natural tendencies you have that might be getting in the way of your performance improvement efforts, then focus on them to overcome them. Carl Jung, the father of human psychology, hypothesized that each one of us is born with natural tendencies or predispositions towards certain personality traits. As an example, each one of us has a tendency towards being an extrovert or introvert. In addition to extraversion and introversion, he introduced other factors to assess personality traits. Many assessment instruments such as the MBTI (Myers Briggs Type Indicator) exist that we can use to assess our natural predispositions.

What the assessment instrument says is that, as an example, if I have a disposition to be an introvert, then I will live my life as an introvert. (By the way, every time I have taken a personality assessment, I have found myself to be a very strong "I" or introvert.) If as an introvert I find myself in a work situation that supports extroverts, then I and other introverts are not going to be very comfortable, and this can impact our performance. This was exactly my experience when I left engineering and got into training and public speaking.

These natural tendencies rule by default, but we can override them and not allow them to limit our performance if we make a determined and conscious effort. Have you seen people who started off naturally as left-handed and because of constant coaxing to use the "correct" hand, the right hand, became ambidextrous? That is, they could use both their hands with equal ease? I have even seen an individual with no hands develop his feet to the point where he could write, paint, and draw so well you could not tell from the drawing that it hadn't been done with his hands. In another instance I saw a person strum the guitar with his feet and sing a song, no different in the outcome than a person doing the same task with his or her hands.

Having clarity of our personal vision, we have the wherewithal to overcome our natural tendencies. With our personal vision comes a sense of direction and a sense of purpose. Now when we find ourselves in situations that do not support our natural preferences, we can generate the internal fortitude to overcome the discomfort we experience and not let it impact our perform-ance. This enhances the likelihood of our success.

Create High Expectations

Program into your mindset high expectations for yourself. You have heard the phrase that children live up to or down to their expectations. So do adults, and we need to create our own high expectations. One way to create these high expectations is to think at a couple of levels above where we are. Three steps to pro-gram these high expectations into your mindset are as follows:

1. *Say your high expectation to yourself to internalize it.*
2. *Articulate it and write it in black and white.*
3. *Share it with others. This is a smaller version of public disclosure and public commitment.*

Goal Setting and Goal Achievement

The ideal situation for creating goals and becoming goal oriented is after you have your personal vision and have set high expectations. Now focus on the details on how to get from here to there, from the present state to a future state defined by your vision and the goals that have become small, specific steps towards your vision. In setting goals, here are some suggestions to maximize the probability of achieving your goals:

- *Make your goals fit the acronym "SMART." This stands for "specific," "measurable," "achievable yet aggressive," "realistic," and "time specific."*

- *Become goal oriented. That is, know your goals, have your goals in front of your consciousness at all times. Be aware of your goals. When you are engaged in an activity, see how the activity connects with your goals. Assess your activity for its fit with your goals.*

- *Make your goals public by sharing them with your business and personal relationships. They become internalized through the process of being shared, and now that they are public, it increases your tendency to want to make progress so you can report progress.*

- *Prioritize your goals. For your vision and specific situation, you should know what the most important goals are and the priorities you attach to each goal. I have yet to hear of anyone tell me that he or she has an abundance of resources such as time, money, or staff. Prioritization of goals helps to allocate scarce resources. Also, if goals suddenly get dropped, it is easy to handle the loss and fill in with the next important goal.*

- *Create a "task and activity" schedule for each of your goals. This schedule will help you identify the critical steps, the milestones, the resources you need, and the resources available and best of all it will help you keep track of your goal completion schedule.*

Time Management

No amount of money can increase the hours in a day. We all have twenty-four hours and no more. How we use the time at our disposal determines who among us accomplishes the most. Some suggestions for the effective management of time are the following:

- *Plan your work activities for that day even before you get to work in the morning. You might do it while you are driving or commuting to work, while in the shower, while having breakfast, or whatever works for you. For me what works best is, before I get out of bed, to spend a couple of minutes contemplating the things I must do in the course of that day. I know some people who do this the night before.*
- *Similarly plan your after-work personal activities even before you get home to make the most of the limited time you have with your family.*
- *Prioritize your activities and distinguish between what is important and what is urgent.*
- *Identify and address your "time-wasters."*
- *Build skills to assertively say "No" to things you feel you should not be doing or things in which you should not be investing your precious time.*

Change Your Perspective of Work

Develop a value-added perspective of your work. The more you see your work as a meaningful part of your life, the more you enjoy it and the more creative and innovative you become. Here are some suggestions as to how you might be able to think about your work as a meaningful part of your life:

- *Articulate how you might talk to your grandchildren about your contribution in your work.*
- *Write down how your work (as part of your organization's business) helps society.*
- *Make a note of how your work is helping people who work with you.*

For all the years you spend in the workplace, think about what you want your work performance to say about you, what kind of legacy you want to leave behind. I like to think that every day we go to work, we are putting a brick in place to build a house we will reside in when we retire. The quality of the house we end up living in is being determined by the quality of our work every day.

Change Your Perspective of Failure

Anytime we try to do more, we take more risks, and when the risks go up, the setbacks or failures increase. So failure is not necessarily bad. Failure in the cause of self-development and performance improvement is good. It just means we are trying to do more. So change your perspective of failure, otherwise by default failure can be perceived as something to be avoided and with that so can "risk-taking." Think differently of failure. Failure is a stepping stone to success. Failure is your source of feedback. Failure tells you that the strategy did not work and that you should try a different strategy to achieve success.

Visualize Your Success

If you can dream it, then you have a dream. And having a dream is the first step to getting there. I cannot tell you how many successful authors have told me that one of the things that kept them going was their dream of signing books for sale in bookstores. I must confess that the same dream has been a motivator for me also. Think about what success is going to look like for you. Make a dream of your success and "dream on."

Focus on What You Control and Influence

In any project, whether at your work or in your personal life such as coaching soccer, softball, etc., you can think of the things that you have to deal with at three different levels. These three different levels are a function of your degree of control and they are as follows:

1. *Things over which you have* absolutely *no control.*
2. *Things that you do not control, but* might be able *to influence.*
3. *Things you* definitely *control one hundred percent.*

While it might look like there is a gray area between the three levels, my experience is that after some contemplation of the things you are confronting, it becomes very evident at what level it belongs. After all, you are the subject-matter-expert in the things you confront in your situation. You know best your level of control and scope of influence based on your perspective. A visual I like to use to illustrate this concept from a practical perspective is shown in Figure 8 below and involves living in a house. In this visual you control everything you do within the house: the interior walls, the fixtures, the furniture, the temperature settings, etc. You have control over some things in your yard, such as the shrubs, the grass, and the trees, yet you are at the mercy of the environmental factors. These might include drought, too much rain, poor soil conditions, etc. Then there is the neighborhood.

Figure 8

The purpose in this visual is to make the following key points:

1. Your objective in life is to build a house that you can enjoy and feel good about.

2. You want to create the best yard to showcase your house, a yard that says something about the house and the owner of the house.

3. Don't spend your time worrying about the neighborhood. Instead, know that if you have truly built the best house and created the best yard that anyone can, the neighbors might be impressed and might use you as their model. But you do not control that at all.

Given the limited time and resources that we all have to contend with, one of the things that differentiates people who are successful from those who are not is that successful people spend their time, energy, and resources on things they can control and influence. Time and energy spent on things we have have no control over is wasted and not available to improve our performance.

Channel Negative Energy into Productivity

A common experience when we get engaged in things that we do not control and cannot influence is that we feel frustration, anger, and paralysis. This is energy lost in a negative way. That energy is an opportunity to enhance productivity.

One way to prevent this energy loss is to enhance your awareness of your feelings and emotions at all times. No sooner you sense that you are spending time on things that are beyond your control and influence then your awareness will sound an alarm that precious energy is being wasted. Regain control of your mindset and thought processes to break the negative cycle and then channel it to productive alternatives for your situation. Focus on the alternatives. Focus on the benefits of the alternatives. This will provide the incentive to channel the negative energy into more productive outlets.

Action Plan

1. *Identify one natural tendency you have that might be getting in the way of performance improvement and identify steps you can take to override the tendency.*

2. *Identify one new "SMART" goal to improve your performance and share it with your colleagues at work.*

3. *Identify one thing you will do to manage time better and to use the time you have more productively.*

4. *Identify one thing you have been spending time worrying and talking about that is truly beyond your control, as well as what you will need to do to not spend time on this item.*

5

Application to Interpersonal Skills

This is my favorite chapter in the book because it has practical application to every person and because it has made a big difference in my life. As good as I thought my interpersonal skills were, I was able to take them to a very high level in my work with fellow trainers and clients, within my training classes, and in my personal relationships. I hope that you find this chapter of equal value.

While I was still in engineering, I observed a few of my fellow managers and I knew there was something in their interpersonal skills that made me perceive them as being very warm. Yet when I analyzed my own skills, I did not sense the same degree of warmth. I definitely was not insulting, rude, obnoxious, or profane. I certainly was respectful of others. After all, I grew up in a school environment that required us to address all teachers and adults by their last names with a "Mrs." or "Mr." in front. So I clearly was respectful, but others perceived me as being aloof, cold, "business-like," and a "to-the-point" person. I was bothered for years with how I was perceived by others when I really meant to be respectful.

After years of observation and study it became clear to me what is it that makes some people more successful and effective in their interpersonal skills. The difference between those with effective interpersonal skills and those who are not so effective is not that one group is positive and the other negative. Both groups are positive in their interactions. What makes one group more effective are the "emotional factors," the ability to sense and respond to feelings.

There was a time several years ago when people believed so much in the predictability of one's IQ (intelligence quotient) as a measure of who will be successful and who will not that it became a yardstick. People would display pride in their children based on their IQ's with comments such as, "My Tommy is doctor material" and the like.

Then several longitudinal studies were conducted that tracked thousands of students with known IQ ratings over a period of several years. The studies revealed that there was no correlation between IQ and probability of success as an adult. A person with a low IQ was just as likely to succeed as a person with a high IQ, and a person with a high IQ was just as likely to fail as a person with a low IQ.

Similarly, in organizations it was found that for a supervisor, manager, leader, worker, or team to succeed, just having knowledge of the functional skills was no guarantee of success. People skills were also a critical component. And within people skills it was what I earlier referred to as the "emotional factors" that were required:

- *How well can you sense the feelings and emotions of the other person so you can respond to those feelings and emotions? This is critical to being perceived as a good listener. Active listening involves displaying empathy and acknowledging the feelings of the other* person. It is critical to defusing a situation fraught with emotions.

- When challenged, how well do you handle your feelings and emotions? How you handle your emotions determines how you are perceived and in turn the nature of the relationship. How emotions are handled when challenged will determine if a situation escalates into a conflict or if a conflict is avoided and the situation is resolved in a manner that maintains the other person's dignity.

- Are you in touch with your feelings and emotions so they can be leveraged in a constructive fashion? If they are suppressed, they fester and surface in a destructive manner. To be in touch with one's feelings requires the skills for enhancing self-awareness.

- What do you believe about yourself and others? If you don't feel good about yourself, it will influence your interactions. If you think poorly about others on the inside, just saying the right things on the outside will not work.

The bottom line is this: To enhance interpersonal skills and the quality of interactions, just focusing on behaviors by itself does not cut it. It takes more than just learning the right things to say and do. It takes self-awareness. Enhancing self-awareness is a key process in self-development, which is the focus in this book. Hence, this is why this chapter has a special value to me. Building skills to improve the quality of my interactions helped me improve in many other areas, such as leadership, coaching, giving feedback, customer service, and building relationships, to name a few.

Building Skills to Sense Your Own Feelings and Emotions

Let us define the distinction between feelings and emotions as a first step. Feelings are anything at the end of the following sentence: "I am feeling ...." Emotions are a characterization of feelings into certain groupings such as anger, happiness, sadness, etc.

Some of the strategies to enhance our awareness of our feelings and emotions so we can use them as an asset rather than let them become a liability include the following:

- *Reflect after each emotion-arousing situation on what causes you to become emotionally aroused and identify the feelings you are experiencing.*
- *At the end of each day do some self-analysis and identify your feelings in the different situations you experienced in the course of the day.*
- *Start to think about and identify your feelings in the moment as you are going through a challenging discussion with another person.*
- *Begin to express your feelings in the moment as you experience them during every discussion.*

Express Your Own Feelings and Emotions to Others

Communicating our feelings to others in the course of our interactions adds another dimension to the message of just the spoken words from the speaker to the listener. While this might enhance the depth of the message, how those feelings are expressed is also just as important. Let me share two different ways of expressing the feeling of getting upset at the tone of a conversation:

Your tone of conversation is getting me upset

versus

I need to let you know that I am feeling a little upset at the tone of this conversation.

See the difference between the two ways of expressing feelings? You might want to reflect on different ways in which you might express your feelings to people in situations you experience. Here are some situations for you to practice:

- *You are having a discussion with your manager about a meeting that you were not invited to. You cannot imagine any other way to think about it than what the facts say and that is that you were ignored and insulted.*

- *You are having a discussion with your partner about the social event that you agreed to and were reluctant to attend because you were afraid you would not know anyone. You and your partner agreed prior to the event that your partner would stay by your side and get you involved in the discussions. That is not the way it worked out at all and you have a right to be angry at your partner. For the three hours you spent at this event, your partner was gone more than half the time having a great time without you.*

Feelings Ignored, Person Ignored

When someone expresses feelings of hurt, sorrow, pain, or joy and the feelings are not acknowledged, it is like ignoring a part of the person. Let me share two examples that come to mind that I have witnessed.

The first example is from the work situation. Once a group of us was in a meeting room at 8:15 a.m. waiting for one of our work group members. She walked into the meeting room in a hurry around 8:25 and the first words out of her mouth were, "Wow, what an accident!" The manager's response was, "Why don't you have a seat and we can get started." In defense of my manager, I must say he was a very nice and positive person, yet there was no question that an opportunity to acknowledge, probe, and respond to feelings was lost.

In the other example I have, I was sitting alone with a woman and her young daughter just making small talk at the dining table after breakfast. The mother said to her daughter, "Honey, what's the matter with you? How come you are so quiet? You look like someone died." The daughter blurted out, "I just hate myself. I am so ugly." With that, the mother with the best of intentions and a desire to help responded, "Now, you know that is not true. You are very pretty." Hiding her tears, the daughter ran to her room upstairs. Once again, an opportunity to probe, and respond to feelings was lost.

Think about your interactions from the last few days and identify what opportunities you had to acknowledge, probe, and respond to feelings that were missed.

Build the Skills to Sense and Surface the Feelings of the Other Person

Having built the skills to sense and express your own feelings is a great step forward. The next step is to sense and draw out the feelings of the other person. This makes the discussion whole rather than limited to the dimension of the spoken words. There are two components to the skill to sense and draw out the feelings of the other person:

> 1. One is the behavioral component, what to say or do, and that is very easy in this situation. It might be a simple question such as, "Tell me how you feel?"

> *2. This is the harder component of the two and is the internal component about "Why should I bother? How he or she is feeling is not my problem. If he wants to share it, no one is stopping him. This is too touchy-feely for the workplace." This is where the motivation to remember and to invite the other person to share his or her feelings comes from. If the internal component to provide the motivation is not there, then all the behavioral skills might not help. And if this component is missing, we need to look for the answers in the self-image or, more specifically, in what we believe about others.*

Some other examples of things you can say to invite the other person to share his or her feelings include:

- *Share with me what your feelings are about this issue?*
- *I see you are upset. Can you tell me what is causing you to feel this way?*
- *Does this decision make you angry?*
- *I care for you and I would not want to make a decision without finding out how you feel about it, so help me?*

The Relationship between Beliefs and Behaviors

A good way to see the relationship between beliefs and behaviors involves children. If you can get a child to believe something, you will see that belief reflected in the behaviors of the child immediately. This relationship was illustrated very well in a video from an experiment conducted with third and fourth graders in the late 1960s. A brave teacher, Mrs. Jane Elliott, conducted the experiment where on a given day she was able to make a group of children in her class feel either superior or inferior based on the color of their eyes. This experiment was captured in a video called

"Eye of the Storm." This relationship between beliefs and behaviors is illustrated in Figure 9 below:

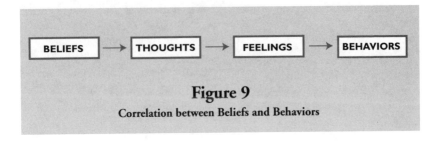

Figure 9
Correlation between Beliefs and Behaviors

In adults this relationship between behaviors that we display and our beliefs might not be reflected at all times. When our beliefs tell us that we should behave a particular way and our actual behaviors are different, we experience "dissonance" or a "disconnect." This disconnect can arise for a variety of reasons. Some might be as follows:

- *The fear of people finding out what we really believe can cause us to display behaviors different than what we would otherwise display if we did not have this fear. An example might be that if I fear I might get laid off, I might not tell my boss how I really feel about a decision. I might pretend that I approve of the decision, when in reality I might believe it is a bad one.*

- *The desire to project a certain image on the outside if we are uncomfortable with our real self-image can impact our behaviors. For example, if I want to project an image that I am a heterosexual when in reality I am not, I might pretend to laugh at gay jokes even though on the inside I might feel offended.*

Being Perceived Genuine in Interactions

When people perceive a disconnect between behaviors and

beliefs, they perceive the person to be phony and hiding something. Genuineness requires that our behaviors reflect what we believe. If we sense a disconnect, the answer should not be to force a behavior change but to examine the beliefs in the self-image.

A simple illustration of this might be from the example cited above. If I have a fear of getting laid off from my job and that is causing me to behave in a way that creates "dissonance," the solution is not to forcibly change the behavior but to do some self-analysis to enhance awareness of the fear and acknowledge the presence of the fear and somehow express the fear. This makes the behaviors appear more genuine.

If we do not go through a conscious process of analyzing our beliefs of other people and addressing them, then by default our prejudices and biases can influence our interactions with others. This can happen without our awareness. Hence the importance of taking time to reflect and analyze the beliefs about others in our self-image. The ultimate objective is to bring ourselves to the point where we truly believe in others as we believe in ourselves, and if we just cannot, then to acknowledge the gap and be aware of it.

The Communication Model

The communication model in its simplest form is illustrated in Figure 10. It consists of the transmission of a message from sender to receiver. Let's say the message is a simple verbal one the sender sends to the receiver.

The sender, based on his perception of his overall self, has his own filters. These filters consist of various senses such as the sense of confidence, sense of esteem, sense of superiority, sense of belonging, sense of direction, etc. These filters will shade the "world view" of the sender and this includes the sender's perception of the receiver. Let's say the message the sender wishes to send to the receiver is, "Don't forget the meeting at 8:00 a.m. tomorrow." The sender is sending a gentle reminder out of caring that the receiver with her busy schedule might forget the meeting. The sender's thoughts are, "I don't know how she manages so much stuff and this meeting can be forgotten so easily, so I will remind her of it. She will appreciate it."

The receiver also has her own filters that consist of her various senses and through those filters has her own world-view. The receiver receives the message, but based on her world-view perceives it as a "sledge-hammer" taunt about the meeting. The receiver's thoughts are, "How dare he taunt me this way? Just because I was a little late for one meeting this year he has to rub it in."

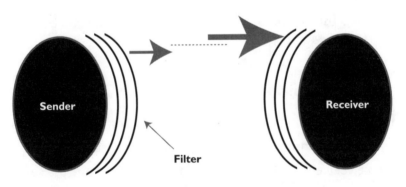

Figure 10
The Communication Model

Intent Versus Impact

One of the many concepts that complicate communications between two people is this one of "intent" versus "impact." "Intent" means our intentions when we say or do something, and by "impact" we mean the impact the message or communication has on the receiver. Let us take another look at the communication model in Figure 10 above to illustrate how this concept can complicate communications.

In our model the sender is sending a gentle reminder about an upcoming meeting to the receiver. The receiver in our model is aware of the following:

- *the message (as perceived by the receiver)*
- *the impact it has on the receiver*

The sender on the other hand is *not* aware of (and cannot be aware of) the impact the message has on the receiver. Instead, the sender is aware of the following:

- *the message (as perceived by the sender)*
- *the "intentions" of the sender in sending this message*

The receiver is not aware of the intentions the sender had in sending the message. This is internal to the sender. Let me illustrate this concept of "intent" versus "impact" with an experience I actually had several years ago. I was facilitating a class on assertive interactions and as was my normal practice I chose a man and a woman seated up front to illustrate through a role-play the difference between assertive and aggressive interactions. During my first break in the day, a participant I knew very well came up and informed me that the man I had selected for my role-play felt offended. I was astonished at the reaction since it had never happened before, and my instinctive internal reaction was, "He is being too sensitive; that is not the way I intended it." Fortunately I was able to meet with this individual during the break and to straighten everything out before resuming class. The learning for me and the point of this story is that no matter how well-intentioned we might be, our interactions can have a totally different impact on the other person than intended.

This experience also illustrates how easily such misunderstandings can happen as a result of this concept of "intent" versus "impact." A solution to avoid such misunderstandings is to inquire what impact our actions might have on the other person. It could be something as simple as, "What is your reaction to the comments I made in our meeting? How did you feel about my comments?"

Strategies for Effective Interpersonal Communications

Holistic Interactions

A human being is very complex compared to even the most complex machine. What makes a human being complex is the presence of feelings and emotions that are not visible at all. What are visible are just the behaviors we observe. Hence our tendency is to react to what we observe, namely the behaviors. We can make our interactions more effective by reacting to the whole person, and that includes beliefs, thoughts, and feelings in addition to behaviors. This is called holistic interactions. The strategy in this approach to holistic interactions is simple: to probe for the feelings and emotions and beliefs driving the behaviors of the other person. Some of the questions for this probing can include the following:

- *What do you believe caused your son to talk back to you in the presence of his friends?*
- *How did you feel when he did that?*
- *How do you feel about your emotional reaction in response to his behavior?*
- *What would you need to do to feel better?*

High Self-Esteem Talk

In every situation there are tens if not hundreds of different ways to communicate something. Of the many ways, which way is the best? A criterion you can use to determine the most effective way of communication is this: Say it such that ideally you enhance the other person's self-esteem or at a minimum maintain the other person's self-esteem.

One way to use this criterion is as follows: Anytime you need to say something in challenging situations or to address an issue, examine a few different ways of saying it and pick the one that maintains or enhances the other person's self-esteem. Here are some ways a first line supervisor might let a worker know he is lifting a salt block improperly and that he needs to bend his knees when lifting to avoid injury:

- *Are you looking for an LTA (lost-time accident) absence or what? Bend those knees before you lift the block of salt. Good.*
- *Please bend your knees as you learned in the safety class when you lift heavy objects. Thanks.*
- *You have a problem, don't you, with remembering the safety training on how to lift heavy objects? I want to see you bend your*

knees before you suffer a back injury. Thanks.

- *You are key to the operation of this place with the quality of the work you do. I hate to see anything happen to your back as you lift the block of salt. So please bend your knees, as you know you should do. Thanks.*

Which option will work and why? Which will help you get the outcome you are looking for? There is no guarantee you will get this outcome, but the likelihood is greater if you use the approach that enhances the other person's self-esteem. In fact, let me repeat that there is nothing you cannot say to someone as long as you say it in a manner that simultaneously enhances his or her self-esteem. How can anyone feel hurt or offended if his or her self-esteem is enhanced?

Think of a situation you face where you need to communicate something challenging to someone. Think of several different ways you might communicate the issue. Then pick the one that comes closest to enhancing the self-esteem of the other person.

Effective Listening Skills

I can remember talking with my teachers in my younger days, standing in their offices as they busily typed away on their typewriters. They listened to everything I said, yet I never felt like they were listening. This had an impact on me: I did not want to say anything more than the minimum.

What a shame. There was a time when good listening meant nodding, eye contact, and listening to someone without interrupting. Not any more. Effective listening skills now refer to being engaged in the communication process to make it active listening, where the listener is actively involved in the process of listening. This means acknowledging what you hear the speaker say. This active involvement sends a message of caring to the speaker that you truly are listening. Active listening also demonstrates that you definitely understand what the speaker is saying. It encourages the speaker to share even more when the speaker feels that the listener cares for the speaker.

Re-Statement for Active Listening

One very effective way to demonstrate that you care is this simple technique of "re-statement." Re-statement means to re-state back to the speaker what you heard the speaker say. Some examples of how re-statement might sound are as follows:

- *So what I hear you saying is that your son was unhappy with the way the teacher treated him.*
- *I am hearing you say that you were barely introduced to the people you will be working with in your new job.*

Clarifying Questions

Another way to demonstrate that you are truly listening to the speaker is to ask clarifying questions regarding what the speaker is saying. This demonstrates an interest in hearing more about what the speaker is saying. Here are some examples of asking clarifying questions:

- *Why don't you tell me more about why you liked the way you managed the meeting?*
- *Tell me what else you did besides sending him the email to have him apologize for not keeping your date?*

Paraphrasing

You can also demonstrate that you are truly listening by para-phrasing. To paraphrase means to say something back to the speaker in your own words. It is like re-statement except more in your own words. Not only does paraphrasing demonstrate that you listened to the speaker, it shows that you also added value to what the speaker said. Some examples of paraphrasing are:

- *I think you are being too generous in characterizing your treatment by your new boss as "not very good"; I think it was just awful. He should be embarrassed.*
- *You are right on. You felt like a fish out of water and they responded very well to make you comfortable.*

Empathy

Using empathy means recognizing and acknowledging not just the words that the speaker speaks but also the feelings and emotions the speaker feels. There are few basic emotions: anger, sadness, happiness, and fear. What is important is that you recognize the emotions in the speaker the way you feel them. What this does is to take interpersonal skills to a higher level, beyond just words and into feelings. There is a clear and distinct distinction between empathy and sympathy. Sympathy means expressing sorrow for what the other person is going through, whether it is a loss in the family or the loss of a job. Empathy means putting yourself in the shoes of the speaker to show understanding of what the speaker is feeling. Sympathy is always expressed for emotions like hurt, pain, and sor-row that result from experiences where you suffer a loss of some-thing. Empathy can be an expression for feelings of happiness or sadness. Examples of empathy displayed in interactions are as follows:

- *It is understandable that you got frustrated when your comment in the meeting was totally ignored.*
- *I can see you felt very bad when the teacher did not look at you and just looked at the boys in the class for the answers.*
- *I see you are ecstatic about how your husband surprised you on your anniversary. I would be ecstatic too if my husband surprised me that way.*

Be Non-Judgmental

To be "judgmental" is to prejudge a situation or a person. Imagine that you are late to a meeting at work because of an accident. As you walk into the meeting room, the manager mentions to you to make sure you set your alarm clock tomorrow so you are there at the start of the meeting. After saying this, the manager leaves the room. This leaves you feeling that the manager is one hundred percent convinced that you overslept. In this case, the manager has prejudged why you were late.

What is the impact on a person when he or she perceives that the other person has made up his or her mind and is not open to your explanation? You feel, "Why bother explaining? The other person is not going to listen anyway." When this happens, people clam up and don't make any attempts to explain their perspective and communication becomes one-sided.

Here are some examples of "judgmental" and "non-judgmental" statements:

Judgmental: Jim, you are a sexist based on the comments I heard you make in the meeting. What do you have to say for yourself?

Non-Judgmental: Jim, some of the comments I heard you make in the meeting did sound sexist to me. Can you help me understand what you meant by them?

Judgmental: Mike, you are such an obnoxious loud mouth, you dominate meetings with your opinion on any topic and never give anyone else a chance to speak their mind, and if they do, you do not hear them.

Non-Judgmental: Mike, you have some rare skills that you can express your opinion on any topic and in the moment. I have a lot of people who do not have that skill. I would love to see you help them develop the skills you have by giving them some space in meetings and inviting their opinions.

To avoid being judgmental in your interactions, use "I" statements to eliminate the possibility of being perceived as judgmental. Let me illustrate with one example:

Judgmental: Joe, your comments about age are sarcastic. Tell me why?

With "I" statement: Joe, when I heard your comments about age, they sounded sarcastic to me. Help me understand?

Avoid Being Directive

A directive comment is one that sounds like and comes across to the ears of the listener as an order. Examples of directive comments are as follows:

- *I do not want to hear you mention that raise you feel you are owed one more time!*
- *If you do not change your behaviors, you are history with this company!*

• *I definitely do not want to see you bring up that item in the meeting.*

There might be situations when directive comments are in order. The criteria I suggest is to ask whether, in any given situation, the communication can be conducted in a non-directive form. If so, the non-directive form should preferably be used. I personally do not appreciate directive comments and I am sure many other people feel the same way.

The impact of a directive comment is that since it is perceived as an order, the recipient of the directive comment is focused more on the process of communication than on the message. Once the process distracts the attention, the likelihood is greater that the message will get lost in the communication process between the sender and the receiver.

I once had a woman in my class share an interesting story about the negative impact of directive statements. She worked as a lifeguard at a swimming pool and one of the things she learned in her training was that when she saw children running on the poolside, she was never to holler out to them, "Don't run." Instead, she was to call out, "Please walk." Supposedly a higher percentage of children respond to "Please walk" than to "Don't run." In fact, she stated that when children hear "Don't run," they actually run faster to complete their task.

Open-Ended Questions

One of the objectives in a challenging interaction is to figure out what is going on internally with the other person. People are walking around with "emotional baggage" that is influencing their behaviors and interactions. To achieve successful behavior change, we need to help "unload" that emotional baggage. A key skill to help unload that baggage is to get the other person to open up and talk about what is on his or her mind. One strategy to get the other person to open up is to ask open-ended rather than closed-ended questions.

A closed-ended question is a question to which the other person can respond with a one-word answer such as a simple "Yes" or "No." Here is an example of a close-ended and an open-ended question:

Close-ended: Andy, do you like working here?

Open-ended: Andy, please share with me what is it that you like about working here.

Assertive Interactions

One way to understand assertiveness is to think "rights," not like in "right" and "wrong" but like in "your rights" and "my rights." Imagine that you are a homeowner with a fenced-in yard, and next door is your neighbor's home with a similar fenced-in yard. Here are some possible things you might consider as your rights:

- *You are entitled to play your choice of music and to cook your own style of food in your own home.*
- *You are entitled to mow your lawn, clean your home, and shovel the snow on your driveway at your own schedule and not necessarily on your neighbor's schedule.*
- *You are entitled to drive the kind of car you like to drive and to wear the kinds of clothes you prefer.*

Here are some examples of rights you might not accord to your neighbor:

- *Your neighbors can play their choice of music, but after 11:00 p.m. the volume must be toned down; then it gets into your sleeping time and you have to get up early.*
- *If the neighbors want to violate the village ban of parking on the street that is their right, but they cannot park in front of your house.*
- *If the neighbors let the snow pile up on their driveway to a height of two feet that is their choice, but they should not use the snow blower in a manner that causes the pile to end up on your driveway.*

While we used the example of home ownership to make the point about things we might perceive as our rights, similarly in interactions we perceive rights we feel we have when interacting with others and we accord rights to others based on our perceptions of them. Now it is easier to define and understand assertive interactions.

Think of interaction styles represented on a continuum as illustrated in Figure 11 with the following key points on the continuum:

- *In the middle of the continuum is the assertive style. This is someone who asserts his or her rights without violating the rights of others. In the instance of the neighbor who has parked in front of your house you might say, "Jim, I know we all park on the street once in a while, but would you mind not parking in front our house? I am saving the spot for our contractor working on our landscaping. Thanks a lot for your understanding."*
- *On the other extreme of the continuum is the aggressive style. This is someone who aggresses on or violates the rights of others. As an example, let's say you observe Jim parking in front of your house*

since you have blocked his driveway, and you comment to Jim, "Jim get your car away from my house. I need to park in front of yours so I can see my car from my house. That's the reason. You need to find another spot for your car."

- *On the other extreme is the submissive style. This is someone who gives up his or her rights to appease others or to avoid conflict. In this instance the man might say to his wife, who is none too happy about having the neighbor's car parked in front of her home again, "Honey, it's not that big of a deal. He'll move it soon enough. Let's just pretend it's not there."*

Submissive   Assertive   Aggressive

Figure 11
Assertiveness

In interactions, the objective is to interact assertively with others. This is successful because by definition it allows you to assert your rights without aggressing on the rights of others. It keeps the rights of others intact. To interact assertively requires an understanding of two things:

1. Clarity of rights of "self," and this comes from the self-image. A person with a poor self-image might compensate by claiming more rights than are appropriate or by yielding most of the rights that appropriately belong to his or her "self" in order to appease the other person. Neither of these two options is healthy and both can negatively impact interpersonal skills. The correct way to identify rights that we should assert is to develop a strong and healthy self-image.

2. Clarity of rights accorded to "other," which also comes from the self-image.

What rights should you accord to another person to generate high quality interactions and a productive relationship? How about this: "No matter what the other person says or does, I will not resort to tit-for-tat. I will always interact in a manner that maintains the other person's dignity"?

When we improve our interpersonal skills, we benefit at many levels. It improves our personal relationships and we work better in teams and improve our interactions in the workplace as well.

Action Plan

1. Analyze your daily interactions for the next two weeks every evening while they are still fresh in your mind. From the analysis of these interactions, identify at least two situations where you wish you had communicated differently, situations where you wish you had communicated in a manner that would have enhanced the other person's self-esteem. Then make up for the lost opportunity by addressing the situation. This might mean contacting the other person and saying something to the effect of, "Yesterday I said something that needed to be said, yet I said it in a way that I don't feel good about."

Once you do this for two weeks, you will start using high self-esteem talk in the moment every time the need arises.

2. Analyze your interactions for use of active listening skills and identify the following:

a. missed opportunities

b. what you would do differently next time

6

Leadership from Within

"**Leadership** from Within" is the term I use to indicate that true leadership starts from within us and flows out through the self and into others. If leadership does not start from within, it is just a display of leadership behaviors that might or might not stand the test of challenges that leaders face.

Creating a Leader–Mindset:
Self-Leadership First, Other-Leadership Next

Creating a leader-mindset starts with beliefs and then plays out in behaviors:

- *Believe you can be a leader.*
- *Think and feel like a leader.*
- *Act like a leader.*
- *Generate specific action plans for your self-development as a leader.*

On the inside you need to feel the confidence and the competence to be an effective leader. When you are convinced about yourself, others will see it. If you cannot convince yourself, how can you convince others?

Once the conviction has been created, identify specific action plans for your self-development as a leader. This does two important things:

> 1. *It builds your skills as a leader.*
> 2. *It makes you a role model for others to engage in self-development. If you are not engaged in self-development and are just focused on others, no matter how good your intentions, you will come across as "preachy," as focused purely on others.*

Characteristics of an Effective Leader

You might want to put down this book for a couple of minutes and make a list of the characteristics of an effective leader that are important to you. Think of the leaders you admire and the kind of leader you aspire to become as you go through the exercise.

In every class I conduct on the topic of leadership, I ask my participants, "What is the one thing you feel makes a person an effective leader?" Some of the many items that have surfaced are reflected below:

- *good listening skills*
- *clear vision*
- *decisiveness*
- *trustworthiness*
- *a caring attitude*
- *being worthy of respect*
- *confidence*
- *passion*
- *not wishy-washy*
- *leads change*
- *hard working*
- *a role model*

As the next step in this exercise, identify those characteristics that are important to you. Then, for each of those characteristics, identify the internal and external component as defined below:

- *What specific observable behaviors will a leader display to demonstrate that characteristic? This is the external component of the characteristic.*
- *What kinds of values and beliefs does a leader need to have for that characteristic? This is the internal component of the characteristic.*

An Example: Good Listening for a Leader

As an example, let us identify the external component and the internal component for the characteristic of good listening skills for a leader.

External component (behaviors). A leader will:

- *use eye contact*
- *nod to show understanding*
- *verbally acknowledge understanding*
- *paraphrase or restate what he or she heard*
- *ask clarifying questions, etc.*

Internal component (values and beliefs). A leader will:

- *not have stereotypes about the other person and thus prejudge the comments*
- *be caring of the other person to be able to focus on the conversation*
- *have built a trusting relationship so the other person wants to openly share*
- *believe that the other person has something of value to say and hence will not tune out mentally, etc.*

Leading from within means not just displaying behaviors, but also having the corresponding values and beliefs that will support the behaviors.

Correlation of Beliefs and Outcomes

Imagine two individuals selling encyclopedias door to door. Both individuals have the same educational background and both have the same work experience and have been given the same training. One person believes the product he is selling can truly be of value to the buyers and the other does not have any such belief. Guess which one will be more successful? The one who has the belief in the value of the product. Think of this as a basic truth: *What you believe will influence the outcome.*

Hence the two basic beliefs about leadership skills that will influence the probability of success in making an effective leader are the following:

1. The person who truly believes he or she can be an effective leader will more likely become one than someone who does not feel as confident, and more importantly,

2. The person who truly believes that every individual reporting to him or her is capable of becoming an effective leader will be more successful in generating leadership in others.

The more I observe organizations, the more I am convinced that the test of an effective leader these days is someone who can create other leaders. This criteria is vitally important as organizations become flatter and more work is done away from the workplace and the need for leaders at all levels becomes ever more critical to organizational success.

Leading from Within through High Self-Esteem

Being driven from a position of high self-esteem influences the quality of leadership in the following ways:

- *You have clarity of personal vision and can align organizational vision better with personal vision and display passion for the organizational vision.*
- *The clarity, acceptance of, and focus on the organizational vision facilitates leadership in organizational change.*
- *You can interact as a leader in a manner that maintains or enhances the self-esteem of others. This improves two-way communication.*
- *High self-confidence flows from having high self-esteem. The high self-confidence in turn facilitates risk-taking without fear of how others might perceive you.*
- *Clarity of your value system helps you become decisive.*
- *Clarity of your belief system helps generate belief in others and makes you more able to display confidence and build leadership in others.*
- *Clarity of belief in others helps in modeling diversity and inclusion to impact organizational culture.*
- *You are engaged in continuous self-development and are able to create a work environment that values learning and growth and uses feedback to this end.*

Leaders Motivate Others

Remember the saying, "You can lead a horse to water but you can't make him drink"? The implication here is that you cannot motivate others and that they have to motivate themselves. What do you believe? Remember this basic truth: Our belief influences the outcome. For myself, I absolutely believe that you *can* motivate others if you understand what needs they have that are not being met.

The obvious motivators that come to mind when we think about motivating others are increasing the wages we pay someone, making an improvement in their benefits, or making some other improvement in the resources. These are examples of external motivators. Now, what if you have improved all these external motivators and their performance still does not improve?

Abraham Maslow, the father of motivational psychology, theorized that as human beings we all have needs and, further, that our behavior is driven by our needs. He came up with a list of needs in hierarchical order starting with the basic physiological needs for food, shelter, and clothing. Some of the higher level needs he identified are the needs for belonging, affection, achievement, and self-esteem, all the way up to the need for self-actualization. As each of these needs is met, he theorized, we feel better about ourselves and about life itself. If we address the lower level needs of people, we can expect performance at one level. If we address the higher level needs of people, they will perform at a higher level.

I had an experience like this shortly after I first got into training. I was doing average work and getting by. I had no complaints about my salary, benefits, or working environment. My participants were rating me a fairly good trainer and I just was not motivated to invest efforts to improve further. I was satisfied with cruising through my job at that level.

Then I got a new manager. He talked with me at length about what a great opportunity I had to have a major impact on people and how I was fortunate to have the skills and the knowledge for the job and that it should be a great source of pride for me.

Over time I saw a change in myself: I wanted to work harder to continuously improve my skills to do even better. I was not doing it because of more money or better benefits or for any external motivators. The motivation for me wanting to do better was purely from the feeling of accomplishment and satisfaction the work itself gave me. This is internal motivation, and it happens when higher level needs are addressed and satisfied. I am sure that you have seen many people so enchanted by a new software product that they spent their own time in their work driven purely by the love of the work itself.

This excitement about the work is not something that only happens at higher levels in the organization or only in work done by professionals. It can and should happen at all levels. A fellow trainer shared a story about doing some training for a company that did some work for NASA. As she was setting up her meeting room for the training, adjusting the tables and hanging up her flipcharts, the janitor walked in to do his cleaning. She engaged in a brief conversation with him about how he liked his work and he replied, "How can you not like it? I am working to send people up to the moon and back. The better I do my work, the better others can do their work and the more likely we will be successful." His reply says it better than anything I can say about the importance of how you perceive your work. His perception of his janitorial work was meeting his needs for survival and more. Hence, work on developing a value-added perspective of your work. Think of all the value your work can have to society and to consumers and then program that perspective into your mindset.

As a leader in an organization, a teacher in a classroom, or a parent at home, we all encounter challenging situations. Anyone can work with someone who is already motivated to want to do his or her best work. The real test comes when we encounter challenging situations. One key to motivate those who might not otherwise be motivated is to figure out what needs they have that are not being satisfied and then to make efforts to satisfy them. The needs might be for belonging, for self-esteem, for achievement, for affection, or for anything else. But I cannot fulfill any need another person might have unless my needs are fulfilled first. The process of self-development involves fulfilling each of these needs first for ourselves through improving our self-image and then we are in a better position to help motivate others.

Strategies to Address Higher Level Needs

Here are some of the things that leaders can do to motivate others by addressing their higher level needs:

1. Reflect on the proposition that "People will perform at a higher level if their higher level needs are met." Bring yourself to the point where you believe in this proposition, because this belief will influence the outcome from your efforts.

2. Think about your own higher level needs to ensure that they are being met. Why? It is very hard to help meet the higher level needs of others if these needs are not being met for the leader. As an example, I cannot make others feel good if I don't feel good going in to work. I cannot make others feel like they belong if I myself don't feel like I belong in the workplace. Likewise, I cannot enhance the self-esteem of others if I have low self-esteem myself.

3. Then analyze your present interactions and identify what needs they might be addressing. Here are some examples of leader-interactions for you to practice and identify what needs are being addressed:

- "It has been a long day for you, but feel good as you go home about what you did. You got the production line running again and at a higher speed than anyone thought possible and it is running smoothly. Have a nice evening."
- "If I don't see a change in your behavior, you will be history."
- "Well, thanks for sharing with me the opportunity you have found at another organization and the salary increase they have offered you. I wish I could say that we can match that. But we cannot. Our pay policies will not allow me to do that since you just got a promotion over here. If you do choose to leave us I will respect your decision and understand. Let me just say that I think you belong here. You are respected and have earned the trust of the senior managers. I cannot guarantee anything, but I do believe that you will see more opportunities come your way and in the long run that this is the place for you."
- "If you want to see a raise of five percent at the annual review, here is what you need to do."
- "You should feel good about yourself. You have some rare skills. I watched you as you interacted with the irate customer and the way you calmed her down. That was great. Thanks."

4. Now that you have analyzed your own interactions, think about what opportunities exist in your work situation and what you need to say and do to address higher level needs to motivate your people. Consider both the interactions you have as a leader with individuals in your work group and also the interactions with the team as a whole.

Value and Belief System for Leading from Within

Imagine two leaders being challenged in an organization with their organizational commitment to increasing ranks of women in the workforce. How each leader will address the challenge will depend on what is in the mindset of the leader regarding the issue. The leader who believes that women are not emotionally suited to be leaders will say the right things outwardly and yet the belief in the mindset will influence the outcomes from the leader's efforts.

On the other hand, the leader who has a belief in the mindset that women can provide the kind of leadership that is desperately needed for the present times will also say the right things outwardly, yet will have a different outcome.

Now here is an opportunity for you to reflect on the questions below and to engage in some self-analysis:

- *What is your organization's policy and practices on issues such as women in leadership; minorities; plant closings; layoffs; same-partner benefits; union organization; diversity; zero tolerance; sexual harassment; racial discrimination; benefits to the number one assets, the employees; social responsibility; environmental considerations; two-way communication in the organization; performance management process; pay equity; education and training opportunities for all; quality of life benefits, etc.?*
- *How do you feel about the stated policies and about how they are carried out? Is there a gap and why?*
- *What are your personal beliefs as compared to the stated policies? Is there a gap and why?*
- *How do your people perceive you about your stand on these policies? As a champion, or something else?*
- *How do you want your people to perceive you? Based on what you believe on the inside or based on the image you would like to project? If there is a gap, how do you feel about the gap?*

Leaders Display Passion for Organizational Vision

Every organization I know has a glorious vision of wanting to be the world leader in health care or food products or in customer service. The problem is not with the vision. The vision provides the glory needed to arouse passion. The question is, can all leaders display passion for the organizational vision? I have seen leaders in the same organization looking at the same organizational vision using the same words and still the difference in their passion was very visible. One just read the words and the other brought the words to life. What makes this difference?

Imagine two leaders, one who has a personal vision for his or her life who is able to align the organizational vision with his or her personal vision. The other leader has no such personal vision and sees the organizational vision as a stand-alone item. Which one do you think will be able to internalize the organizational vision and display passion for it? And what is the source of our personal vision? It comes from within us, from our self-image.

Types of Personal Visions

Let me share with you a range of personal visions and then you decide which of these would allow you as a leader to align your organizational vision with your personal vision. On a continuum here are some possible personal visions:

1. *For me life has no meaning at all; it is just one of those chance things.*
2. *My personal vision is to retire as soon as possible to a nice warm place in Florida.*

3. My personal vision is to help my children in their education so they can achieve their potential.

4. My personal vision is to learn and grow and develop myself to be able to achieve my potential and also to help my family achieve their potential.

5. My personal vision is to learn and grow and develop myself to be able to achieve my potential so I can help my family and others beyond my family to achieve their potential.

For me personally, the higher up I am on the continuum ladder of personal visions, the easier it becomes.

Risk of No Personal Vision

The power of having a vision is best evident in the situations where, unfortunately, there is absolutely no vision. As young people growing up at home and going to school, we are dependent on our parents to provide the personal vision through role-modeling that sense of direction. If that does not happen, it leaves a void. In this vulnerable age period, especially the young teen years, that void can create a sense of "purposelessness." If that is not addressed, it can even lead to suicide. Or, equally bad, that void can get filled at school with a vision that provides a negative sense of purpose. This in turn can lead to behaviors where our youth risk their lives and the lives of others.

Test of an Effective Personal Vision

A personal vision has to meet some criteria to be of value, otherwise why bother developing one? As you work on developing your personal vision, think about some of the leaders you admire and the personal visions they might have had and how these visions might have helped them in their personal and professional lives. The leaders I admire are Mahatma Gandhi, Henry Ford, Mother Theresa, Bill Gates, Nelson Mandela, and Viktor Frankl. Here are some key criteria that I feel a personal vision should meet:

- *The longer the duration the better; ideally the personal vision should transcend life as did Mother Theresa's.*
- *The personal vision should allow you to anchor your organization's vision with your personal vision.*
- *Your personal vision should help you stay focused on your personal and professional goals.*
- *Your personal vision should help you cope with the challenges and frustrations every day brings in your personal and professional life.*
- *Your personal vision is something you should feel good about today, tomorrow, and on your last day of life.*
- *The quality of the vision should lead to an outcome you want. As an example, did Hitler have a vision? Yes he did, and a strong one. However, the outcome of his vision was the Holocaust. Visions based on perceiving some groups of human beings as inferior to others leads to negative outcomes.*

The ultimate test of a vision is the outcome that the vision will generate. Religious fanatics have a vision that drives them, and the outcome from their vision often involves loss of their own life and the lives of others. Hence, a vision that generates an outcome that we think of as positive will be a vision that values all human beings, a vision that involves service in some form. It might be service to children or the underprivileged, or service through art or building monuments that will inspire generations to come.

Leader–Mindset for Effective Delegation

Analyze the work that you do and ask yourself, "Is there some-one in my group who can do this job?" or "Is there someone in my group who can do this work with a little coaching?" If the answer to either of the preceding questions is "Yes," then the fol-low-up question is, "Why am I unable to delegate?"

Then use your responses to the questions below to build delegations skills:

1. *What concerns or fears do I have as a "delegator"? Could they be any of the following:*
   - *The other person might not do as good a job as I can and might make me look bad.*
   - *The other person might do a better job than I can and might make me look bad.*
   - *If I delegate this job, I might not have enough work to do myself.*
2. *How do I address this fear?*
3. *What does the "delegatee" need to be able to do his or her best work? What do I need to do to support the "delegatee?*
4. *How do I reprogram my mindset to become more effective at addressing the needs of the "delegatee" and start delegating like a leader should?*

Leaders Are Decisive

This characteristic of decisiveness for effective leaders comes up often in my talks. Let us analyze this characteristic in the behaviors an effective leader might display to exemplify decisiveness and the leader-mindset that might support a leader to be decisive.

Some of the behaviors a decisive leader might display are the following:

- *thinking through complex problem situations and making decisions in a timely fashion*
- *not procrastinating to an undue extent*
- *not displaying excessive fear or frustration in making decisions*

Now let's examine the mindset necessary to support the ability to be decisive in the workplace. From my personal experience, I know that my ability to be decisive was enhanced substantially after I gained clarity of my personal value system. Can you see two leaders in the same job, one who has clarity of his or her value and belief system and the other who has not gone through the process of gaining such clarity? Which one of these two leaders will be able to be more genuinely decisive in the workplace?

This clarity of one's value system and belief system comes from within, from the self-image. Some additional things in the mindset that help a leader to become decisive are the following:

- *high self-esteem, so the person is not worried about, "What will others think if I make the wrong decision?"*
- *high self-confidence to minimize the fear of taking risks and the fear of insecurity*

Leaders Display Self-Confidence

Leaders who are self-confident are respected. How is this characteristic of self-confidence developed? First let us understand what self-confidence is and what it is not. Self-confidence is not the following:

- *having all the answers*
- *not displaying any fear*
- *never making a mistake*

On the other hand, behaviorally, self-confidence is often displayed in many opposite behaviors such as the following:

- *The self-confident leader is not embarrassed to display vulnerability and his or her fears.*
- *The self-confident leader can acknowledge not having all the answers and can acknowledge mistakes when mistakes are made.*
- *The self-confident leader can take the heat when mistakes are made and can still rally the troops to do what needs to be done.*
- *The self-confident leader freely asks for feedback. The self-confident leader is not fearful of negative feedback and receives feedback well.*

What kind of a leader-mindset does it take to display self-confidence? The answers lie in understanding what self-confidence is:

- *Self-confidence is nothing but a feeling.*
- *It is a feeling of competence.*
- *It is a feeling of "I can."*

It is a feeling of, "This is the right thing to do. I am not worried if it fails. I will not do things differently because of how others might perceive me."

Leaders Display Confidence in Their People

If you have gone through some self-analysis about your people and have brought yourself to the perspective where you truly believe in your people, then you can display confidence with ease in them. By displaying confidence, you can inspire self-confidence in the other person to go the extra mile and to put in that extra effort. Sometimes the other person wants to put in the extra effort so as not to disappoint you for the confidence you placed in him or her. Anytime you are trying to address an issue with another person, add a comment about genuine confidence you have in the other person.

Here are some examples of how confidence can be displayed in another person:

- *I know that you have the skills to participate in meetings and have some creative ideas to contribute. I am not seeing any participation and that is what I want to talk about. I just do not want to lose ideas that you have in our discussions.*
- *You clearly are qualified to do these computations, and that is why these errors I am seeing are so surprising. I am one hundred percent confident that you can correct all the errors once we understand why they are happening.*

I had a promotion opportunity once to become the manager of an engineering group and sadly, eight months into the job, it was not going well at all and I had my letter of resignation typed up and was looking at other opportunities. Fortunately, the job market was very good. Just then a major organizational change took place, my manager got promoted, and I got a brand new manager. This new manager sensed that things were not going well with me and also had received comments from the previous manager. Within three days after he came on board, he had a conversation with me about my performance and here are some of the confidence-boosting comments he made to me towards the end of our fifteen-minute discussion:

*I understand and sense your frustration with the work here and the
undeserved negative feedback you feel you have received from your
internal customers. Let me tell you what I do know about you: You
know this plant very well; you know the processing, the packaging.
You know your engineering, you are very respectful in your interactions, and no one can accuse you of not being hard working. Why our
customers are not satisfied I don't know, but I will be darned if we
cannot figure it out. Go home, have a nice weekend, and let's talk
about it next week.*

Well, when I went home that Friday evening, I was reconsid-
ering my thoughts of resignation. When I went to work on
Monday morning, I had my resignation letter all torn up. And
good thing I did. The situation worked out. In fact, it worked out
so well that years later when I did leave that company, I left with
the idea that I would love to go into training to teach people how
to manage people. One comment I must make in defense of my
previous manager: He was a nice manager, not insulting, and had
no biases that I sensed. I behaved the same with both the managers. What made the difference was their belief system.

Displaying Confidence in Others:
The Indirect Approach

An even better approach to display your confidence in one of
your people is to use the "indirect approach." In this "indirect
approach," you talk to others and let the positive comments sneak
back to the particular individual from other channels such as
peers, other managers, customers, etc. Now the feelings in the

individual on hearing the positive comments of confidence are, "My manager must mean it to have shared it with others. I better work hard and make sure I do accomplish the goal."

This approach works equally well with children at home. Let your child's friends know how proud you are of your child's sense of responsibility and sense of caring, both in the classroom and out. Comments that we receive indirectly that were originally not intended for us have very high credibility. When we receive the same comments directly they can be suspect with the feelings, "Is there a hidden agenda here?"

Leaders Inspire

This characteristic of being able to inspire others is assessed more by how others perceive us. Others feel inspired when they feel "elevated." It starts with how the leader feels about his or her work and the goals the leader is pursuing. If you as a leader can elevate your goals to a higher moral purpose within your own mindset, that elevation comes through in your communication about those goals with your people.

I have experienced this feeling from both sides, as an employee and as a leader. As an employee, I have worked for both less and more inspiring leaders, and as a leader myself I have been less and more inspiring also. I will share the experience where I worked for two different leaders in the same situation. When I first got into training, I had leaders who spoke their minds about having to deliver training programs on diversity that we would be undertaking for our client organizations.

The less inspiring leaders communicated this work through

addressing the concerns of trainers (such as I was at that time) by making the following key points:

- *The participants in your training class are mandated to attend this program, so be prepared for seeing a display of negative attitudes.*
- *If you experience a display of extremely negative and offensive behaviors, you can have the participant leave the class.*

By contrast, the more inspiring leaders that I had prepared us trainers for the same clients and addressed our concerns by making the following key points:

- *This is a great opportunity to deliver a program that we all believe in and that is part of our mission.*
- *It is understandable that some participants might come in not wanting to be in your class since they are being forced to attend.*
- *Your challenge is to show empathy for their feelings and gradually turn them around to where they feel this class was worth their while.*
- *I have confidence in your skills as trainers to be able to accomplish this. And you also have the choice to ask a participant who in spite of your best efforts is disruptive to leave the class.*

Guess what? With the approach of the more inspiring leader, we trainers did not have to ask one single participant to leave our classes. The inspiring leader elevated the goal to a higher level and in the process inspired us to elevate our efforts. This type of leadership is also referred to as "transformational leadership."

Take a look at the goals you are leading your people to and how you can elevate them to a higher moral level. Re-state the goals and try them out on your team.

Leaders Turn Around the Poor Performer

The biggest challenge to a leader and the acid test of leadership is with the employee who is performing at or below average level. Once again, what is in the mindset of the leader will influence the outcome.

Imagine the outcome a leader might have with the following assumptions about a "poor" performer in his or her mindset:

- *The poor performance has been there for over a year.*
- *I have been patient with the employee and have offered to help, but I don't see any commitment to want to change.*
- *This person's previous manager had the same feelings that this employee was not motivated.*

Now imagine another leader with different assumptions in the mindset about the same "poor" performer:

- *Despite the comments from the previous manager, there is no reason why this person should not be able to deliver a much higher-level performance.*
- *This person has the knowledge and skills to do good work, so my expectation is that the person should deliver work up to that standard and no less.*
- *I will create the expectation of good work and display confidence in the person to be able to deliver to our standards.*

Neither mindset is visible on the outside. What is visible on the outside are the behaviors, what the leader says and does. And yet in the behaviors there are subtle clues that suggest what might be in the mindset.

Leadership at All Levels

Does your organization really believe there is a need for leaders at all levels? If so, what is the organization doing to create leaders at all levels? Hopefully, at a minimum, the employees are provided leadership training, they observe role modeling within the organization, and they experience a culture of responsibility and accountability.

Let me give just one illustration of the impact on the organizational productivity when workers can see the work they do as a value-added part of their life. Imagine two individuals working in a candy factory. One worker sees the work as a stand-alone part of his life. He thinks of work as "something you have to do to make money so you can do other things you want to do." The other worker sees the work as a meaningful part of his life. He thinks of work as "an opportunity to continue to do what makes my life meaningful. I make candy products that kids like and hopefully it will keep them away from drugs and other things that are really bad. To that extent my work will help kids and I feel good about it."

Now imagine if every employee in your organization felt this way about whatever work he or she did for the organization. If every employee felt like a leader, what impact would that have on your organizational productivity?

Leaders Think Change

Whereas a manager might look at a complex task and think, "How do I simplify this complexity for execution," the leader looks at the same complex task and thinks change: "How do I change our current way of doing things to the new way of doing things?"

When a manager sees a complex task such as "ABC," the manager breaks the complexity down into the manageable chunks "A," "B," and "C" for execution. A leader on the other hand sees the present way of doing things as "abc" and thinks, how do I change that to "ABC"?

How we perceive things influences our subsequent strategies. For the leader it leads to an awareness of the present state, an assessment of the desired state, and from that a vision of the future. Once again, having a personal vision allows the leader to anchor the vision of the organizational change, to generate passion for the change, and to display that passion with the work group. The leader has taken the "business case" for the change and created a "personal case" for the change.

A leader who is driven from within is focused on securing that "buy-in" of the people based on the "business case" and the "personal case" the leader makes for the change. And with the focus on securing the "buy-in," use of leader-authority does not arise. Instead, the key is influencing skills based on arousing passion for the vision.

The key steps in making change happen successfully include the following:

1. *Create dissatisfaction with the present state or situation.*
2. *Develop clarity of the future state or create a vision.*
3. *Create a business case for the change.*
4. *Create a personal case for the change for yourself and for your people.*
5. *Present the above to your people.*
6. *Jointly develop the strategies to get from the present state to the future state.*

7. *Develop shared responsibilities for the implementation.*

8. *Implement the strategies.*

9. *Conduct a periodic review of progress and make corrections as dictated by the situation.*

10. *Follow up after the change for next steps.*

Based on my observations, most organizations excel in steps 2, 3, 5, and 8. Most organizations based on my observations fall short on steps 1, 4, 6, 7, and 9. The one step where I think skills most urgently need to be built is in making the personal case for the change initiative. The best way I heard a CEO present the personal case to his people was as follows: "Forget me and forget the organization for the next hour. Let me tell you why you should want to make this change happen for yourself..." And he listed about five to six reasons while making the personal case and it worked very well.

Test of Effective Leadership

A good test of effective leadership is when you do not have to use authority to influence people to perform. Leadership, when effective, is displayed in the quality of the "followership." When leadership is inspiring, people *voluntarily* want to follow the leader, not because of a dependency relationship on the leader. Effective leadership is voluntary and not coercive.

Leaders Create a Work Environment
That Is Productive for All

Leaders think "big picture" and think "long term." You do not want to be a leader to eighty percent of the people. You want to be the leader of *all* the people. The whole objective of building leadership skills is more than just to provide effective leadership within your work group. If the sports team is losing the game, no matter how effective the leadership of the defensive coach, it doesn't count for much. Make your leadership count by constantly assessing your organization's strategy, structure, operations, and practices to improve organizational productivity.

I am confident you will find many opportunities in your work situation to use your leadership skills for a positive impact on your organization, and maybe even to create your legacy. Let me share with you some thoughts I have to get the process started:

1. *Create an inclusive work environment. A productive work environment is one in which every employee can contribute to his or her potential. The underlying philosophy is that if employees do not feel included in the workplace, they will not quit. They will continue to work, yet they will not do their best work. For employees to do their best work, they must feel included. When they feel included, it fulfills their sense of belonging. This is a very important higher level need on Maslow's hierarchy of needs.*

Here are some suggestions to ascertain the quality of the environment in your work situation and to make it more inclusive:
- *Use employee surveys.*
- *Create an open environment and seek feedback from employees on how they perceive the work environment for inclusion.*
- *Have employees identify items that might be causing them to not feel included.*
- *Prioritize items and generate action items for your execution.*

2. Create inclusive policies and practices. Examine your organization's policies and practices to ensure they are not inadvertently making employees feel excluded. As an example, consider the manner in which recognition might be given to employees for extra effort. I have seen this recognition communicated with the most sincere intentions yet in a manner that caused others in the work group to feel excluded. With that in mind, examine how policies might be executed to maximize inclusion of all employees.

3. Assess your organization's long-term survival. Leaders think strategy and think long-term. No matter what level you are at, engage in thinking about things you could do to ensure your organization's long-term (twenty to fifty years) survival.

Action Plan

1. Use one of the change initiatives you are currently working on and use the steps in this section to execute the change initiative.

2. Identify two leadership skills you need to build to become a more effective leader.

3. Identify one task you are currently working on that can be delegated and go through the analysis of why it has not been delegated. Follow up the analysis with delegation of that task.

4. Identify from discussions with your work group two things you can do to make the group more inclusive and cohesive.

7

Stress Management

Why do two people with similar educational, financial, and family backgrounds react so differently to the announcement of an upcoming organizational re-structuring? One person becomes stressed out and experiences anxiety attacks, while the other person handles the news in stride and even sees it as an opportunity to learn and grow.

Why do two people in similar challenging relationships react to the situation so very differently? One person is unable to walk away from the relationship and suffers through putdowns and abuse for years on end, while the other person is able to walk away from this relationship and build an even better one elsewhere.

Your computer might crash and create a headache for you, yet your computer experiences no stress. We human beings should be so lucky. For us, to live is to experience stress. So the choice we have is how we react to it.

It's All in Our Perception

The approach in this book is not to work on eliminating those situations that might be stressful for us. The approach in this book is to understand that what makes a situation stressful for each one of us is how we perceive that situation. The situation is emotionally neutral. It's how we react that makes the situation stressful. The core of this book is that we control our perceptions from within our self-image. We can shape how we perceive situations so that instead of perceiving them as very stressful, we can perceive them as less stressful or maybe even as opportunities from which we can learn and grow and develop.

Some Stress Is Unavoidable

If you have an important meeting to attend and, despite your best efforts to be there an hour before the meeting starts, you find yourself running late, it is normal and natural to feel tense.

If you lose a near and dear member of your family, experiencing grief and stress as a result of the loss is once again normal and natural.

Stress Can Be Constructive or Destructive

The loss of a young child is stressful on all parents. Yet when the stress reaches the point where it leads to suicidal tendencies or all interest in living is lost or when the resulting quality of life becomes a burden on others, the stress has become destructive.

The same situation can create stress that has a constructive outcome. It might be in the form of a commitment to appreciate each living day and to value every child for the capacity and potential that every child possesses.

Small Stressors Can Lead to Big Stresses and Vice Versa

There is no scientific correlation between the intensity of the stressor and the magnitude of the stress experienced. Have you seen people who reacted to a very small event such as spilling coffee with an intensity that appeared totally out of line with the event?

I have seen a situation where a friend of mine, after being rear-ended and pushed into oncoming traffic and ending up in the hospital with serious injuries through no fault of his own, responded by saying, the first thing out of his mouth when I visited him, "I am blessed. Thank God I was all alone in my car. I am happy for that."

The big events such as death, divorce, job loss, and bankruptcy are stressors to be sure, but they are not necessarily the major stressors. It is the cumulative effect of the little things that over time can become the major stressors that cause individuals to snap and do things out of proportion to the last stressful situation.

Happy Events Can Cause Stress
Just the Same As Unhappy Events

Along with unhappy events such as death, divorce, and job loss, happy events such as a promotion, moving into a new house, retiring, and being married can also cause stress. Once again, what makes an event stressful is much less the event and much more how we perceive the event.

One Source of Stress: Poor Self-Image

Any inadequacies in the self-image, if left unaddressed, can magnify and lead to an inferiority complex, which in turn can lead to stress. This can play out in many different ways, including the following:

- *Constant comparison to others with thoughts such as, "I am not as good as John" or "I wish I were like Jamie."*
- *Envying others.*
- *Anger at parents, at society, at Mother Nature, or at God for the inadequacy.*
- *Investing time and efforts to create and project a different image and then becoming frustrated when it does not work.*

No matter how the inadequacy plays out, it leads to dissatisfaction with the existing "self" and to stress. The answer to this stress is in Appendices A, B, and C. First we must identify the inadequacy, then work through the process to address the inadequacy, and finally we must build a stronger, healthier, and more positive self-image. This is one big source of stress. Another source is our expectations.

Our Expectations and the Stress We Experience

A good way to illustrate the relationship between our expectations and the stress we experience is with this simple situation: Let's say I come home and my wife tells me, "Guess what? Your ship has finally come in. You have the winning ticket to last night's lottery. I checked and re-checked and all the numbers match."

I am excited about the news and check the numbers for myself. Sure enough, they all match. I am beside myself and begin planning my next steps: resigning from my present job, moving into a bigger and better house, and more. I carefully and securely take the ticket to the drugstore and they take one look at the ticket and inform me that I have certainly won, but this was not the big weekly lottery but the daily lottery and my winnings are $10,000. I will experience a certain level of disappointment from this situation.

Let's replay the situation above with a small twist. I come home and my wife tells me, "Guess what? Your ship has finally come in. You have the winning ticket to last night's lottery. I checked and re-checked and all the numbers match." I check the numbers myself to make sure they all match. I feel lucky to have won anything at all and it would be great to celebrate with a nice dinner. I take the ticket to the drug store and they take a look at the ticket and inform me that I have certainly won $10,000 in the daily lottery. I am excited with the winnings and tell myself, "This will buy us more than just a few good dinners. I am truly fortunate." I will experience a certain level of gratification from this situation.

In both the situations above the outcome was the same, namely winning $10,000. Yet one situation created disappointment and the other situation gratification. What generated the different emotional reaction was not the outcome but the expectations from within. In most situations in real life we cannot control the outcome, but we do control our expectations and to that extent the stress we experience.

While the difference between the outcome and our expectations determines if we will experience stress, the magnitude of the difference between the outcome and the expectations will determine the magnitude of the stress. The greater the difference between the outcome and the expectations, the greater the stress. This concept is illustrated in Figure 12.

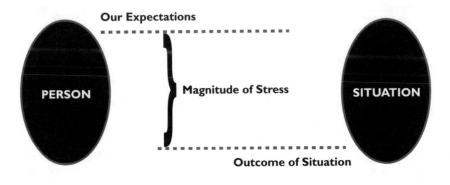

Figure 12
Determination of the Magnitude of Stress

Let me play out another situation to reinforce this relationship between our expectations and the stress we experience. Let's say you studied hard for an exam that you must pass since your livelihood depends on it. Your expectation is that you will get an "A" for all the hard work you've put in from early morning to late night preparing for the exam. You are disappointed when you get your results in the mail and find that all you got is a "C."

Let's replay this same situation with a twist in your expectations. Your expectations now are that you would love to get an "A," but you would be delighted to just pass and move on. You open the envelope and find that you got a "C."

You will experience a different level of stress in each of these situations. In each one, the outcome is the same. What is different are your expectations. The outcome in many situations we do not control, yet we do control our expectations.

Strategies to Minimize Stress

Program Your Expectations to Minimize Destructive Stress. Develop real world expectations for situations you are involved in. Let me illustrate what I mean with a situation I experienced. I once was a manager of an engineering group when, because of the increasing workload, I hired an engineer for my group. I made it a point to have high expectations for this individual and communicated these expectations to him. Despite my best efforts to elicit a quality performance, the engineer turned out to be a major disappointment. This situation became very stressful.

Years later I had the opportunity to hire another person to work in my group. This time I also had high expectations, as any manager should, but I also had real-world expectations: I knew I could not control how the person might perform or the character the person might bring into my department. This person accused me of something that was determined to have no basis, yet I handled this situation with less stress because of my real-world expectations.

Create Real-World Expectations. Let me tell you the story one of my participants shared with my class on stress management. She was experiencing a high degree of frustration with a colleague she worked with on a team at her work. She had gone out of her way to help train her colleague when he was newly hired. Now that he was trained and they worked together as colleagues, he was not showing the appreciation she expected for all the help she had provided him early in his career.

As she was sharing the story of how frustrated she was, she looked at me and said, "And where did I get the right to expect that just because I was nice to him, he would be nice to me? You know, that is my problem. It is my expectations that created my frustration. Suddenly I don't feel that frustration as much as before I came to this class."

I think this story says very well that often it is our expectations that create our stress.

Analyze stressful situations from your recent past from the workplace and from your personal life. See what expectations you had in these situations. Then ask yourself the question, "Where did I get the right to have that expectation?" Enter the situations that you come up with in your journal.

The Risk of Rigid Expectations

Often I will hear people ask me, "Are you telling me I should not have high expectations for my children? What happened to that saying that children will live up to their expectations?"

Well, I'm really not saying that you cannot have high expectations for your children or for the people in your organization. What is being proposed here is that just to have the high expectations and nothing else leads to rigid expectations, and there is a risk of stress and frustration when well-intentioned high expectations are not met.

What is therefore needed is a balance for the high expectations we create. Having real-world expectations provides this balance. Without this balance, we tend to perceive the only set of expectations as a threshold. Either the expectations are met or they are not, and it becomes a win-lose situation.

Now analyze stressful situations that you are currently experiencing. Analyze your expectations. If you have high expectations of someone you are working with or someone in your personal relationship, continue to have your high expectations but along with them, simultaneously create real-world expectations. Now if the worst-case scenario is the outcome, you will not be as devastated as you would be otherwise.

<u>Examples of Real-World Expectations</u>

Here are some examples of real-world expectations that, when programmed into the mindset, can proactively reduce the stress you might experience:

- *There is no guarantee that just because I am nice to someone he or she will be nice to me in return.*
- *Life is not fair. I might be the more qualified candidate for the promotion or job, but I still might not get it and there might not be anything I can do about it.*
- *In a relationship, I might be very considerate and respectful and yet the other person might not be trusting of me. I will just need to keep working at it and build the skills to make it work if I still want the relationship.*
- *I might work very hard and do everything I'm responsible for and more, and my boss still might rate me as no more than average. I will need to keep building the skills to deal with it.*

- *I might be a very good and conscientious teacher and all my students and most parents and fellow teachers recognize my passion, but if one or two parents think I am awful, I will just need to deal with it.*
- *I cannot control what others believe, think, or say about me; all I control is how I react to it, and how I react is a function of my self-image.*

This strategy of creating real-world expectations worked very well for me in my training work. I encountered many situations where for certain organizations or certain programs the participants in my classes were mandated to attend by company policies. Many of them came into my training programs with an attitude and showed it in class by refusing to participate. This became extremely frustrating for me. And then I used this strategy of programming real-world expectations into my mindset. I repeatedly told myself certain things and came to believe them. Some of the things included the following:

- *They (the participants) have a right to come in with their feelings.*
- *I have to build the skills to deal with them.*
- *I should build the skills to tap into their feelings, debrief their feelings, show empathy, and try to enlist their participation.*

Guess what? This strategy worked very well. Not only did my programs get better with this strategy, I enjoyed them much more. It reached the point where these participants that I previously used to dread now actually added value with their participation.

Develop Clarity of Personal Vision. If life is a journey, what is a journey without a destination? Remember the Cheshire cat in "Alice in Wonderland" inquiring about which road to take at the fork and being told, "If you know not where you are going, then it matters not which road you take"? To me the definition of a lost soul is "a person on the journey of life with no destination."

I know from my own experience when driving a car that when I am lost and have no clue which way to go, I feel the stress. For this reason, drivers are much more safety conscious and drive defensively when they are driving towards something they are looking forward to such as a wedding, a graduation, a date, or visiting family. Drivers who get on the road just to vent their frustration with no particular destination in mind or drivers with a destination they are not looking forward to are more likely to take greater risks and to drive in an unsafe manner.

Having clarity generates passion, a sense of purpose, and a sense of direction. It provides a reason to live and live well because there is good reason to want to get to the destination. The person with this sense of purpose and direction can withstand the stresses and frustrations that arise in the workplace better than someone lacking that sense of purpose. Having that sense of purpose provides a reason to deal with the challenging situations rather than fight them at all levels.

The personal vision provides meaning to living. Viktor Frankl in his book *Man's Search for Meaning* says, "The primary motivational force for man is his search for meaning." This becomes the driving force in life.

Having clarity of your personal vision gives you the ability to put the everyday stressful situations you encounter into a big-picture context. The situation becomes reduced to something very small, not deserving of your time or energy to worry about it.

Build Physical Health and Fitness. Building your physical health and fitness has benefits at multiple levels:

- *At one level you work off the negative emotions experienced when you are under stress.*
- *At a higher level you are building the physical and physiological conditioning to cope with the stresses you will experience in the future.*
- *At a still higher level you are reinforcing your priorities and you stay more focused on taking care of yourself by spending time on things that help you rather than spending time worrying about the unfairness of life and the people who cause your stress.*

Use your personal vision for motivation to get engaged and stay engaged in a regular fitness routine. You would not embark on a long journey without making sure you had tuned, serviced, and filled your automobile with gas. The journey and the destination provide you with the motivation to want to get your car ready for the journey. Similarly, in the journey of life the vision of the destination provides the motivation to keep your body in the best shape possible for the journey. Remember that woman whose story I shared early in this book? Her sense of purpose came from her daughter. Your sense of purpose comes from your personal vision. This personal vision transcends life and will last forever.

Nourish Your Body. We've all heard the phrase, "You are what you eat." To me it is like building a house. For a good quality house, you have to use good quality materials. Similarly, to generate the kind of body that will last you a lifetime, design your eating style to provide nourishment for a lifetime.

Improve Your Mental Health. Staying engaged in the process of continuous self-development helps in maintaining our mental health. Numerous studies have been conducted with elderly people on levels of engagement and their impact on brain cells. In one study, an experimental group of elderly people was kept engaged with simple exercises, puzzles, and games. The control group of elderly people was allowed to maintain their normal family schedule. Both the groups were tested over a period of months to study the impact of level of engagement on brain cells. The studies clearly demonstrated that the less-engaged group suffered a greater loss of brain cells that became inoperative. Becoming and staying engaged in the process of continuous self-development has a positive impact on our mental and physiological well-being.

When the mind is engaged productively, it spends less time and energy worrying about things that can cause stress. Staying mentally engaged in activities that help you learn, grow, and develop actually benefits the brain. Fewer brain cells become inactive, and some studies even point towards the generation of new brain cells and memory improvement.

Use Your Value System to Prioritize Challenges. Having clarity of your value system provides a sense of priorities and a sense of right and wrong. Now if a challenging situation arises in an area that is not a high priority for you, it allows you to put the situation in perspective. De-prioritizing a stressful situation reduces the stress. "If the situation is not that important, it cannot hurt me that much."

Apply the Spiritual Perspective. Gain clarity of your spiritual self in your self-image. Now you have the ability to view stressful situations in the world from a totally different level. What is important at one level probably has no significance at all at another level. I know from my own experience that on many mornings I will get up having thought all night long about an upcoming important meeting and my role in shaping it. And then the fifteen minutes I spend in meditation allows me to put the meeting with all its significance in a perspective where I am actually looking forward to it. I come out of my meditation with the perspective that "This meeting will be fun. I will do the best job possible and let's see what happens."

Express Yourself. Talk it out; express what might be ailing you. Express your thoughts and express your emotions. This relieves the pressure that builds within from holding thoughts and feelings unexpressed. For some people such expressions might not come easily. Yet this is a skill, and by definition a skill can be learned.

If you're not normally expressive, trying to become expressive only when you experience stress might not be easy to do. Hence this skill is best built by practicing being expressive at all times. Start building the skill by talking things out first with people with whom you are comfortable, and then extend the practice to all interactions.

Build a Network of Support. The best therapy for dealing with stressful situations is to talk. The ability to talk about your stressful situations has benefits at multiple levels:

- *It vents the frustration.*
- *It defuses the emotions.*
- *It helps you think at a rational level.*
- *It helps you shift your focus from stressful situations to other things.*

In your workplace and in your personal life, build a network of support.

Use Humor. How can anything that makes you feel good not reduce your feeling bad? Humor has the ability to make you feel good. The notion that humor might actually produce healing-enhancing changes in the body is gaining respect among some scientists in a field called "psychoneuroimmunology," which studies interactions between the brain and the body's disease-fighting immune system. While stress can inhibit the body's immune system and make people prone to illness, humor just might have the opposite effect.

The ability to see humor in everyday situations requires a disposition to find the humor and more importantly the ability to not have any hang-ups or sensitivities about the self. This comfort with the self requires a strong, healthy, positive self-image.

Relax. A great yet simple stress-buster is the ability and skill to relax at any time the need arises. To build the skill so that it is available when needed, start practicing your favorite relaxation exercises first in a disciplined fashion. Like any skill that is practiced repeatedly, the ability to relax can become a habit and can be recalled for use when needed.

My favorite relaxation exercises include early morning meditation and deep breathing. During the course of the day when I feel stress coming on, I periodically take a few minutes for relaxation by closing my eyes and practicing deep breathing and dispelling all thoughts from my conscious mind. This works wonders for me. Find your favorite exercises and turn the skill into a habit. Some other relaxation methods that you can consider for their calming effect or to elevate the mind to focus on the finer things in life include the following:

- *music*
- *lighting such as sunlight simulators, lava lamps, etc.*
- *bio-feedback instruments*
- *fish tanks*
- *screen savers on your computer*
- *stress-buster toys*
- *paintings, drawings, pictures of scenery, sculpture, and other art forms*

Use Assertive Interaction Skills. If your stress is caused by the inability to say "No," the prescription is to build assertiveness. This inability to say "No" might be due to different reasons:

- *not having the behavioral skill*
- *something within you that is keeping you from displaying the behavior (this "something within" can be culture or a complex)*
- *an inner desire to please others*

If it is the behavioral skill that is lacking, the skill can be developed with practice. If the behavioral skill is not being displayed because of a hang-up within the self-image, the problem needs to be addressed at the deeper level from within the self-image.

Help Others. The best illustration of the value in caring for others comes from studies done on the beneficial impact of pets on people. Companionship from pets has been found to have therapeutic value in the healing and recovery of patients in hospitals. Extend this to the next level beyond pets to human beings. Compassion for others and efforts expended to help others does several things:

1. *It takes the mind off our own stressful situations.*
2. *It fills our mind with good feelings from having helped others.*
3. *It enhances our confidence in handling our own challenging situations, because if we can help others and make them feel good, we certainly have the skills to help ourselves.*

A reporter once asked the renowned psychiatrist Dr. Karl Meninger, "What would you advise a person who has just lost everything he or she valued in life?" Dr. Meninger replied, "I would advise the person to find someone else in need and help the other person." This is the import in the therapeutic value to the "self" from helping others.

Take a Break. The "fight or flight" approach does not work in dealing with stressful situations, because the stressor is still there to be confronted another day. However, if the regular grind of daily stress has taken a toll to create wear and tear that needs to be healed, a break away from the scene or a vacation often works wonders to provide the rejuvenation to address the stress anew. It can be something big like taking a vacation or something as small as taking a couple of minutes right on the job and transporting yourself mentally away from the work situation. I like the practice of stealing yourself away for just a couple of minutes, closing your eyes, and imagining a situation that is stress-free. Alternately imagine a situation where you have to confront your worst-case scenario and you "look it in the eye." Now when you open your eyes and return to the work situation, the worst-case scenario is not as threatening anymore.

Embrace and Change Negative Stress to Positive Stress. Here the focus is not just on building the skills to cope with the stress that comes our way but on going a step further and welcoming challenges and the resulting stress as opportunities to learn, grow, and develop. Think of stress as the spice of life. We all have seen people and some of us might be in that group that actually works better under pressure, whether that pressure comes from a tight time schedule or from the boss.

Getting to this point where you welcome challenges that come your way and don't allow them to become stressors requires a focus on continuous self-development. This commitment to continuous self-development is generated from having a personal vision. How does this commitment to continuous self-development help develop that perspective whereby you actually welcome challenges? I will ask you the same question I ask participants in many of my seminars: "Assume for a minute that I want to build good facilitation skills. Where do you think I will be able to build those skills? In classes that are easy or in classes that challenge me?" The answer always is, "In classes where I am challenged."

The rationale is similar with all of us. If we are committed to continuous performance improvement, real growth occurs through challenges in the workplace. My growth as a facilitator came when I did not avoid classes that could be challenging and instead embraced them. Similarly for you, think about the challenges you face and start to embrace them.

Here are some suggestions for the process: Identify the challenges you face and tell yourself, "These challenges are there and I will accept them and build the skills to cope with them. If I can cope with these challenges, I can cope with others that will certainly occur in the future."

Distinguish Between What You Control and What You Don't. Identify those things that are a source of frustration for you and then examine those sources to see if you have any control over them. If you determine that you have no control, then the appropriate self-talk should consist of two points:

1. *"I refuse to worry about something that I truly do not control."*
2. *The reasons why it is beyond your control.*

So, as an example, if I am fretting at the airport because I will not make my meeting with my client, appropriate self-talk for my situation might include the following: "I did make a reservation for a flight early enough, and I feel good about that. I cannot control the change in weather that has caused the delay. I checked alternate airlines and they are delayed just the same. Driving is not an option. Hence, I just have to let the client know that I will not make the meeting and not worry about it anymore."

Action Plan

1. What opportunities do you see where you can become more assertive and say "No" to things that you should not be doing? Build and use your assertive skills in the opportunities you identified.

2. Analyze one or more stressful situations you are currently experiencing. Look at your expectations. If you have high expectations of someone you are working with or of someone in your personal relationship, continue to have high expectations but simultaneously create real-world expectations. Now, even if your worst-case scenario occurs, you will not be wholly devastated because you will have been somewhat prepared. Write down the real-world expectations that you generate.

3. Identify the sources of stress in your personal and work life and then see if they are within your control or beyond your control. For those you determine to be beyond your control, create the appropriate self-talk for why you should not worry about them.

8

Soaring to Your Potential

Did Michael Jordan know before he became a champion that he was the greatest? If he had not believed he could be the best, could he have become the best?

Could Muhammad Ali have become the greatest without believing he could be the greatest? Obviously the answer in this book is that the belief influences the outcome. In other words, your belief about your potential will determine what you accomplish in your life.

Defining Your Potential

With an automobile, potential might be expressed in terms of MPG (miles per gallon) or its top speed. A computer's potential might be expressed in terms of its memory, speed, or some other factor. How do we express or define potential for human beings? The best definition I have heard for human potential in your chosen field and in your personal life is, "How far can you go with what you are blessed?" In other words, considering what you have to start with, what is the most that you can accomplish?

Think Differently

Life is more than just something we have to get through. It is a journey we are fortunate to be going through. Think about the "legacy" you want to leave behind, your "footprints in the sands of life," and think about what you want your life to say about you long after you are gone. How would you want all the people you will touch in your personal and work life to think about the impact you had on them? As the great Viktor Frankl extolled us, think about the meaning of your life for you. You need to define your destination to make your journey meaningful. And then you need to set goals to work your way to your destination.

For the prime time of your life that you spend in your work, your work should be more than just something to make money to survive. It should be an opportunity to maximize your contribution and to make your life even more meaningful.

When you think about the United States or Canada, where will future productivity increases nationally come from? Not from working longer. We in the U.S. and Canada are working harder and longer than any other country in the world. Future productivity increases will come from looking at life and work differently. Through looking at life and work differently, we will be driven to become more effective and efficient to make our work and life more meaningful.

Shaping the Mindset

If our beliefs about our potential influence our accomplishments, a logical question to ask is how do we shape those beliefs and create the necessary mindset? One thing is certain: The person who believes, "I can only go so far because I do not have what it takes to go any further" will not go any further. Once we create our own boundaries, we set our limits. Only we can remove our boundaries. Here are some suggestions:

- *Plant the belief in your mindset that your potential is greater than anything you can realistically imagine possible.*
- *Believe that you have all the brainpower you need for what you are doing and then some. Think about the brains of geniuses such as Albert Einstein that have been medically analyzed and found to have used only a tiny percentage of their total capacity.*
- *Create a vision that transcends life. A vision that is accomplished within a life span suggests to me that the vision did not reach far enough.*
- *Set high expectations for yourself in everything you are engaged in.*
- *Constantly search for ways to become more productive, more effective, and more efficient.*

Think at a Higher Level

Start by thinking at a higher level about what you can accomplish and then set stretch goals. Will you achieve the stretch goals that you set in this process? Maybe yes, and maybe no. The outcome does not matter. No matter what the outcome, you will get farther than you would have otherwise. Here are some generic suggestions for thinking at a higher level that you can make specific to your personal situation:

- *If you are a worker in an organization, think about how you could do things two levels above where you are currently.*
- *If you own your own organization, how can you improve the lot of your employees two-fold, which will show up in your organization's productivity?*

- *If you are a manager, how can you work your way to becoming the CEO through demonstration of your great leadership skills within your work group?*
- *If you are a CEO, how can you have an impact on "citizenship" nationally? What might be some obligations from a standpoint of "social responsibility" that you can take to a higher level?*
- *If you are fortunate to be in a position where you can have an impact on "citizenship" nationally, how can you replace the spirit of "nationalism" with the more uniting spirit of "globalism"? What obligations do you have as a leader to leave behind a world that is much more unified as a "single humanity" than split into multiple "nationalisms"?*
- *If you are fortunate to have worked a productive work life and are enjoying retirement, then first of all best wishes on your retirement. Hopefully the needs for achievement and self-esteem that we all have are being fulfilled through the activities you are engaged in. However, if those needs are not being fulfilled and one part of you is yearning for fulfillment of those needs, then let me encourage you to seek opportunities where you can be productively engaged and can contribute. There is a potential resource in our retirees that can be tapped to benefit society.*

Go Forth to Find Your Potential

I hope that a year from today as you look back at the preceding twelve months, you feel very good about what you have accomplished and how far you have come. I hope you feel that you have accomplished much more than what you thought possible just a year ago and find yourself confidently looking forward to the next year. Finally, I hope that this book has played a part in helping you focus on your potential, but the efforts in your accomplishment are all yours. You should feel good about that. My wishes are for even more success to you. When you succeed, others around you succeed. Our world will be a better place thanks to people like you.

Action Plan

1. Enhance your self-awareness about your potential. Visualize the greatest accomplishment in your field of interest that you can imagine. Now identify three reasons why that accomplishment is truly possible if you make the effort.

Appendix A
Establishing a Baseline for Your Present Self-Image

The objective here is to engage in self-analysis and to develop a baseline for the components in your self-image. (You might want to use your journal to record your work on understanding your self-image.)

Where are you now on the scale of self-image? Imagine a scale of "1" to "10" as illustrated below, where "1" represents a "poor self-image" and "10" represents a "strong, healthy, positive self-image."

1 |‾‾‾‾‾‾‾‾‾‾‾‾‾‾‾‾‾‾‾‾‾‾‾‾‾‾‾‾‾‾‾‾‾‾‾‾| 10

Poor Self-Image
*(Don't like the way I see
my overall "self")*

Strong, Healthy, Positive Self-Image
*(I would not change one thing about
my overall "self")*

Self-Image Scale

This involves taking stock of your present program and reviewing each component in your self-image and that is what we will do here. Record your feelings as well as the actions and thoughts you have.

1. Identification of Your Personal Vision

Complete this sentence: My personal vision is ...."
(If nothing comes to mind for this component, fine. The objective here is to simply establish a baseline for this component in your self-image.)

2. Value System

Reflect on and make a note of the things that you value and are able to live with in your life. Also identify things that others value that you do not that cause conflict in your life.

As mentioned earlier, values may be difficult to identify since they operate under the surface. In this case, reflect on your behaviors and you might see clues to the underlying values that influence your choices. Also, as you examine your behaviors to identify the underlying values, pay attention to those experiences that cause you stress. There might be a conflict in values causing this stress. As an example, if I value timeliness and I am always where I am supposed to be well ahead of schedule, and if I am in a relationship with someone who does not value timeliness like I do, that can be a source of conflict.

Here are some ideas to help you reflect on things you do and do not value:

- *work ethic*
- *timeliness*
- *use of profanities*
- *display of sexuality in attire, make-up, etc.*
- *viewing porn on the Internet, movies, videos, etc.*
- *fitness, weight, height, etc.*
- *loyalty at work, in personal relationships, in marriage, etc.*
- *smoking, drug use, alcohol use, etc.*
- *abstinence versus pre-marital sex, etc.*

3. Belief System

Identify beliefs you hold that you feel good about and beliefs you hold that you do not feel as good about. Again, use the following list as a starting point:

- *role of government in taking care of people who are unable to care for themselves*
- *accumulating excessive wealth*
- *social responsibility of organizations*
- *abortion*
- *police brutality*
- *racial profiling*
- *prostitution*
- *medical system: government obligations, organization obligations, etc.*
- *organized unions, etc.*

4. Perceptions about "Self"

The objective here is to identify for each of the sub-components a few items that make you feel good and a few items that constitute inadequacies. The sub-components include your perceptions of your physical self, mental self, physiological self, social self, emotional self, spiritual self, and sexual self. If you're not sure where an item belongs, it does not matter as long as it is identified and reflected in writing.

Use the generic list below to create a list that is specific for your situation. And for each sub-component identify the positives and the negatives:

Ex. Physical Self:

+ *love the hair*   - *nose is too big*
+ *height*   - *teeth, yellow and gapping*
- *tummy, big and sagging*
- *varicose veins*
- *fat thighs*

Ex. Mental Self:

+ *logical*   - *take more time than others to process information*
- *unable to participate in meetings like others*

Ex. Physiological Self:

+ *good stamina*   - *embarrassing body odor*
+ *no allergy problem*   - *high blood pressure*
- *high need for urination*
- *profuse sweating*

Ex. Social Self:

+ *very respectful*   - *awful at first impressions*
   of others   - *introverted*
- *poor at building relationships*
- *feel jealous of others who are considered more attractive*
- *compare myself a lot to trim people*

Ex. Emotional Self:

+ *good at keeping*   - *keep stuff bottled up*
   things inside   - *unable to express feelings*
+ *highly self-confident* - *get emotional when alone*
- *frequent self-doubts*

Ex. Spiritual Self:

+ *have clarity about*   - *clueless*
    life after life   - *a lost soul*
+ *I am somebody*
    important

Ex. Sexual Self:

+ *happy with spouse*   - *have to hide my sexual orientation*
                   - *keep dreaming about other partners*
                   - *embarrassed about sexual organs*
                   - *past prime of life*
                   - *have feelings of inadequacy*

5. Abilities and Accomplishments

Identify those abilities you have and things you have accomplished to date that you feel good about as well as those you don't feel so good about. Here are some thought starters:

+ *computer skills*   - *public speaking*
+ *complex problem*   - *not comfortable with small talk*
   solving   - *receiving negative feedback*
+ *physical stamina*   - *being competitive*
                   - *hard to be patient*

On a scale of "1" to "10" rate how you feel about your accomplishments in many areas that are important to you. Also identify the reasons why you rated yourself the way you did. Here are some thought starters:

• *financial status*
• *social status*
• *political status*

- *planning for retirement*
- *accomplishments*
- *education*
- *being respected by others, etc.*

6. Potential

Identify thoughts you have regarding how far you think you can go in becoming successful.

+ *can do anything I want*   - *born loser*
- *not sure what I want*
- *don't see the light at end of tunnel*
- *have more than my share of problems*

7. Perceptions about Others

As you think about other people, identify the positive and negative perceptions you might have of them. While the thought starters below are generic, make yours specific to other groups and to individuals in your personal and work life.

+ *love people*   - *others are not to be trusted*
+ *everyone can do*   - *most are lazy*
  a great job   - *people are cunning*
+ *everyone is just like me* - *some groups are not as smart as others*
- *others just have good luck*
- *hate to see others successful*

8. Expectations

Identify and write down expectations you have about life, about others, and about yourself. At this point you do not need to assign any value, positive or negative, to the expectations. It might be easier to identify expectations you have after you experience some disappointment or frustration, then analyze what might have been the expectations that caused the disappointment or frustration. Here are some examples:

- *If my nineteen-year-old daughter wants to live with me, I expect her to live by the rules I lay down.*
- *I expect life to be fair. For example, people who work harder should be compensated more.*
- *I expect to get a good job after I earn my degree.*
- *I expect people I pay to do their best work.*
- *I expect people to be loyal and honest.*
- *If I confide in my friend, I expect him to be trustworthy.*

Assessment of the Self-Image

Now go back to the self-image scale at the start of this action plan and respond to these questions:

- *Where would you place yourself on the self-image scale of "1" to "10"?*
- *Why did you place yourself where you did? What are some of the big hang-ups or inadequacies in the self-image analysis that stand out for you?*

In the upcoming appendices, one of the things we will focus on is addressing those inadequacies, and you will also see information on the process to address those inadequacies.

Appendix B
The Process of Continuous Self-Development

With ever-improving computer technology, keeping your computer up-to-date is a life-long process. Similarly, our self-development is a life-long process. In Appendix A you established a baseline for how you perceive your overall self. In this section I want to share with you the process for taking your existing self-image and developing it into a strong, healthy, positive self-image.

The process we will use to create a strong, healthy, positive self-image for ourselves involves the following steps:

1. Identify those things in each component that you perceive negatively. As an example, say in your physical self that you have a hang-up with a double chin and also with wrinkles on your face. Also let's say that in your mental self you have a hang-up with not having the level of education you would like to have.

2. Identify the options available to address those items you perceive as negative. The options concerning the wrinkles and the double chin might include make-up or surgery. In the case of the feeling of inadequacy regarding your level of education, there might be many more options to consider, including going to a college for a degree program or learning over the Internet as part of CBT (computer-based training) or learning on your own through books from the library and research over the Internet.

3. Identify the cost and impact associated with each option. The impact might include the time required to get the hang-up fixed, side reactions, other complications, etc.

4. Review the options available and decide for your situation the most attractive and affordable option. In your analysis, consider how important it is for you to fix the hang-up at the cost involved.

5. Implement the option you have chosen.

If you follow these steps, one of your hang-ups has now been successfully addressed. This should show up in an incremental improvement of your self-image and higher self-esteem.

Addressing Inadequacies That Cannot Be Fixed Externally: Changing Your Perspective

For those items in your self-image for which there are no practical or acceptable options available and yet the items constitute a major hang-up impacting your self-image, the only solution is to change the perspective with which you see that inadequacy. The objective in this approach is to take what is a liability in your self-image and in the ideal situation turn it into an asset.

This process is a lot like re-programming the computer to improve its performance. The specific steps in the process are the following:

1. *Acknowledge the inadequacy.*
2. *Generate the motivation for self-development based on personal vision.*
3. *Re-program the mindset.*
4. *Define long-term and short-term goals based on personal vision.*
5. *Focus on continuous self-development.*

Let us take an example of something that cannot be easily fixed externally and work through the process. As an example, consider a middle-aged woman we will call Rita who suffers from an inferiority complex because she was raised with constant put-downs about her intelligence and was treated with little or no respect in the relationships she has had so far and who does not feel very good about her accomplishments in life.

Step 1: Acknowledge the Inadequacy

As a first step, it is important to acknowledge the feeling of inadequacy. Without this acknowledgement, the tendency is to blame others for this feeling. Once blame is assigned to external sources for the feeling, then the solution can only come from the external sources that created the feeling. Yet since the only source for the solution will be from within, it is imperative to acknowledge the existence of the inadequacy. Some specific ways for Rita to acknowledge the inadequacy would be to express the following statements:

- *I was treated in an awful way growing up and that is terrible. Other people displayed the terrible behaviors and that speaks poorly of them. However, only I am responsible for the feeling of inadequacy and only I can rid myself of that feeling.*
- *The people with whom I had a relationship displayed shabby behaviors towards me. That speaks about their character and not mine, but I am responsible for my feeling of inadequacy and only I can rid myself of that feeling.*
- *In fact, I am better than any of those people in my past and once I get rid of that feeling of inadequacy, I can discover the fine person I am.*

Step 2: Generate the Motivation for Self-Development Based on Personal Vision

A key step in creating change requires a reason or motivation, and the best source of motivation is from the personal vision. In order to develop a personal vision, Rita will need to spend quality time reflecting on what the meaning of life is to her. She will need to talk with people around her who appear to have that sense of direction, that sense of purpose. She might read books to help form her thought processes. Once Rita has defined her personal vision, she can generate the motivation for change.

At the end of the process, Rita will be able to articulate her thoughts about her personal vision. This is a life-long process and the clarity of the personal vision can be continuously reviewed and refined. Let us say that the initial personal vision Rita has developed can be articulated as follows:

"I know that despite the shabby treatment I have received that I am a good person on the inside and I want to prove to myself that I am much better than I was made out to be by others. And then I would love to do something to help other women who have experienced situations similar to mine."

Step 3: Re-Program the Mindset

Once Rita is able to acknowledge her feeling of inadequacy and to generate the motivation from within to change, the biggest milestone has been crossed. Now it needs to be firmly programmed into the mindset. The process for taking what is perceived as a liability and changing the perspective so that it can be perceived as an asset includes three key steps: acknowledging, writing, and sharing. These steps are repeated over and over with new information added on to what is being acknowledged. With repetition of these steps, the new thoughts become part of the belief system in the self-image.

1. Rita will continue the process of acknowledging the inadequacy by just thinking the thoughts in step one above and gradually taking responsibility for the "feeling" part of the inadequacy. She will continue thinking about it to prove that she is not running away from that feeling. She will continue to think about it until the thought of the inadequacy does not become paralyzing and impede her in her work.

2. Now that Rita can think about her feeling of inadequacy with ease, she will move on to the next step: Writing it down in black and white on a paper in her journal. This writing is just for Rita and is not intended for anyone else. As an example, she might want to jot down the following: "Yes, I have been suffering from a feeling of inadequacy. I am not ashamed of it. I will come to grips with it and move on to prove that I am a much bigger person with lots more capabilities and skills." She will do this every day until there is no more discomfort in writing about it.

3. The next step in re-programming the mindset is to share it with others. Rita will share her feelings with her close friends. When the opportunity arises, Rita will share all the feelings she experienced as part of the inadequacy. If this leads to a display of emotions, fine. This sharing can even be done in writing.

4. Finally, Rita will start changing the perspective of how she perceives that feeling of inadequacy. Instead of feeling bad about it, Rita will tell herself, "I will trump that inadequacy. I will not only overcome it, I will use it as a challenge to propel me to greater heights." With these new incremental thoughts, Rita will repeat the process of acknowledging, writing, and sharing until the new thoughts are firmly part of her belief system.

Step 4: Define Long-Term and Short-Term Goals Based on the Personal Vision

Rita now has the personal vision and the motivation and in this step she defines the long and short-term goals that will help get her to her vision. Since the goals are aligned with her personal vision, Rita will be excited and will put forth her best effort to achieve the goals.

Some possible goals that Rita identifies might include the following:

- *meeting people through networking and joining social groups*
- *going back to school and taking classes in communications, business writing, and computer programming*
- *working hard at her present job to succeed and build confidence*
- *looking for more challenging opportunities to make her work more meaningful*

Step 5: Focus on Continuous Self-Development

Nothing breeds success like success. Having successfully taken what was a debilitating item in her self-image and changing the perspective so as to enable growth and self-development, Rita has tasted the success of her abilities. Now Rita knows that if she can do this with the major hang-up in her self, she can do it with other hang-ups. Gaining clarity of her personal vision is the first step for Rita to get engaged in the process of continuous self-development. She focuses on all the components of her self-image. As her self-esteem increases and she feels better about herself, that feeling of inadequacy is now becoming part of her past and her focus now is on the future. Each day brings incremental improvement in one of the components of her self-image and leads to an incremental increase in her self-esteem. Rita is now engaged in continuous self-development. There are other challenges to overcome and more growth to occur, and life is good.

A Few Comments of Caution

In my illustration of the process above Rita was very successful. Will this process work similarly in every situation? Let me share a few words of caution designed to temper expectations:

1. It is very possible that even in the situation above Rita might regress after riding high for a year. The thoughts of the same inadequacy might resurface. So what? It is not the end of the world. Rita now knows what she needs to do and can start the process of re-programming her mindset.

2. It is also possible that after trying this approach for a very long time the inadequacy will still periodically resurface to get Rita down. Even in this situation, it is better for Rita to engage in this process than not do anything and allow the inadequacy and inferiority complex to fester. The bottom line is that even if the outcome is not exactly what we might dream of, it will be better than otherwise. We will be better off for having engaged in continuous self-development than not.

Using the analogy of the computer, I liken these complexes that tend to negatively impact our growth and development as a virus. The tools in this section are like an anti-virus program. This is something we need all the time in our computer. Similarly, engagement in continuous self-development is a life-long process to reach our potential.

Examples of Other Inadequacies That Can Be Similarly Addressed

I cannot think of any inadequacy that cannot be overcome from within. Some of the many inadequacies that can be successfully addressed with this process are the following:

- *I wish I were born with a different ethnicity. The way I was born is a handicap.*
- *I hate this stuttering I have.*
- *I am embarrassed about the way I look.*
- *The abuse I suffered growing up caused all the problems I now have.*
- *I was not smart enough to go to college when I was young. Now I am older and it is too late to try. I'm stuck with who I am.*
- *People are judging me and talking behind my back because I am obese.*
- *I have worked hard for forty-two years and what do I have to show for it? Nothing. Financially I am nowhere and I have no accomplishments I can point to with pride. At work, I am just a worker.*

Building a Strong, Healthy, Positive Self-Image

Now it is your turn to get engaged in the process of continuous self-development. The end result of the process is to have a strong, healthy, positive self-image and high self-esteem and self-confidence.

The process involves starting with the baseline you identified in Appendix A. Now you will go through each of the components of the self-image and identify how you want to shape the various components to make you feel better about yourself. What do you want each of the components to say about you?

1. Create a Personal Vision That Propels You Forward

Vision can be defined as a picture of how you see your destination. I have yet to meet a person who has not experienced that "cry for meaning" growing up who did not ask questions about "Why are we here?" and "Where do we go after this life?" Not every individual has received a meaningful answer or in some instances any answers, so those thoughts have been suppressed. Here is the opportunity to go back and answer those questions with the outcome of creating a personal vision. The value of having a personal vision is this:

- *It provides a sense of direction.*
- *It provides a sense of purpose.*
- *It provides the wherewithal to cope with the setbacks and frustrations we all will experience as part of living.*
- *It helps improve many skill areas such as leadership, coaching, managing conflict, building relationships, goal achievement, and so on.*

Some suggestions on how you might identify your personal vision are the following:

- *Read books, and there are many, to get ideas on personal visions that spurred others to greatness. My favorite is <u>Man's Search for Meaning</u> by Viktor Frankl.*
- *Reflect on what you want your life to say about you after you are gone. What "legacy" would you want to leave behind or what "footprints in the sands of life" would you want others to see about you?*
- *Speak to others who are driven about what motivates them.*
- *Think about people you admire and what might have motivated them. My favorites for their personal visions are Gandhi, Henry Ford, and Mother Theresa.*

Some examples of personal visions might be as follows:

- *My life to me is just to have as much fun as possible.*
- *My vision is to build a nice nest egg and retire to a nice warm place to golf, swim, and eat good food.*
- *My vision is to lead a good and moral life.*
- *My vision is to raise a family and make sure they are taken care of with regards to their education and employment.*
- *My vision is to identify my unique skills and build those skills to the best degree possible and use them to help myself and others develop their unique skills.*

These are just examples for you to get started. I do not make a value judgment on what is a good vision. You make it for yourself. The objective is to identify a vision that will stand the test of time, last you a lifetime, and most importantly provide you with a sense of purpose and the drive to cope with the setbacks and frustrations that will certainly come your way.

The final outcome from your reflection, reading, and talking should be a statement comprised of one to three sentences starting as follows:

"My personal vision for my life is.............................."

As mentioned earlier, this is a life-long process and you can revise your personal vision as often as you like as you gain increasing clarity about it.

2. and 3. Identify Value and Belief Systems You Feel Good About

Our value and belief systems are not something we are aware of. They are formed by default from a young age. One way to identify our value and belief systems is to analyze our behaviors and see what the underlying value and belief systems might have been to influence those behaviors. Another way to identify our value and belief systems is to go through a conscious process to create value and belief systems that enhance our feelings about our overall selves. Let me give you some examples from my situation of the value and belief system I have created for myself, and then you can work on yours:

- *Years ago when I was a first line supervisor, my every other word was a profanity. Then, when my daughter was born, I did some self-analysis about the kind of father I wanted to be. I made a conscious*

decision that I would communicate positively with others no matter
how others might communicate with me. I am happy to report that
I have been able to honor my decision very well over the years and
feel very good about it. This is an example of my value system.

- When I first got into training, I started with facilitating diversity
seminars at a large organization. As part of conducting the seminars,
we shared with the class the organization's non-discrimination
policy. The policy included statements against discrimination based
on race, gender, ethnicity, and sexual orientation. Based on my
upbringing, I had a discomfort with discussions generated in the class
pertaining to sexual orientation. Many in the class had a similar discomfort with the same group. I had to do some self-analysis and
question the basis of my belief. I decided that belief was not valid for
me anymore and I changed it. This enhanced the quality of the
discussions in the seminar and they became more genuine. This is an
example of my belief system.

Now it is your turn to do some self-analysis and start the
process of identifying your value and belief systems. No matter
what you have determined as a baseline for your value and belief
systems, they are not stationary. Rather, they are constantly evolv-
ing throughout your life. Here are some statements to get the
process started:

- Let's say your kids are involved in some mailbox vandalism in your
neighborhood. No one suspects your kids, but you know the truth. Do
you come forward to acknowledge the truth and face the
consequences along with your kids?

- You are provoked into an emotional interaction by another person
and say something you wish you had not said. But the other person
provoked you. Do you apologize, and why or why not?

- You are working out of the house and every week you have to turn in your time sheets to your manager. What is the level of accuracy you will use? Now you are a manager and you have someone you are paying to work from his or her house. How do you react to the same standards the other person uses for the time sheets?

- You are checking out at the grocery store and when you get to your car to load your groceries, you find something substantial for which you have not been charged. How do you react?

- You feel that you did not get the percent raise that you deserved. Do you let these feelings be reflected in the quality of your work?

- You have a business servicing garage doors. You respond to an urgent call by a woman for emergency help on a Sunday. The woman knows nothing about garage doors other than that her door is not working. You find out very soon that the only problem is the door sensor. It has lost its alignment, which should not take any more than two minutes to reset and check. What do you do? (Most of the contractors responding to this call in a televised sting operation created non-existent problems to justify high charges.)

- What do you believe about your religion? Do you believe that yours is the only true religion?

- What do you believe about people in general? Can people be trusted? Do you believe that some groups can be trusted more than others? Do you believe some groups have a higher work ethic than other groups?

- Can you buy into this value system: "No matter what another person says or does, I will address the issue in a manner that maintains the other person's dignity. Otherwise it will not speak well of my value system."

- How important is it to you to put in "face time" where you work?

- You have heard about reporters going to prison rather than revealing their sources of information. How well do you keep stuff shared with you in confidence?

4. Hone Your Perceptions about "Self"

For those inadequacies you identified in Appendix A regarding your perceptions of "self," the objective is clear: You now have a process in Appendix B to address those inadequacies. Here the focus is to take the perceptions of "self" to a higher level. What is a good target regarding each of these components? Let me share some thoughts for your consideration on some sample components:

Mental Self: At the end of your reflection, you want an outcome where you feel (even if you do not have all the education or skills you would like) that you *can* learn and *can* build the skills that you need to advance in your work. Once you end up with this outcome, your perception becomes an "enabler" for your self-development rather than a "debilitator."

Spiritual Self: This is a component that is often overlooked as a source of inner strength for self-development. This component is part of our self-image to help us think of life at a different level. You might want to reflect on this to see to what extent you want to use it. I use the term "spiritual self" in the broadest sense possible to include much more than just religion. Let me share my own thoughts purely as thought provokers for you to develop your own:

- *This life is a blessing and I need to make the most of it to make it meaningful.*
- *There is a life after this life that is even more meaningful. It allows me to put this life with all its challenges and frustrations in perspective.*
- *I came into this world with nothing and will leave it with nothing. Everything I have acquired in the process is pure profit. So what*

counts with the capital I acquire during my lifetime is how I use it.

- *When I think at a higher level, even my family is really not "mine." Hence I will think about my family as a blessing, as a gift for me to enjoy, cherish, and help develop with the skills I have.*

- *If I think honestly, I do not control anyone in this world including my family. All I can aim for is to influence others. All I control is how I react. And I need to be clear on what I want my reaction to say about me.*

- *Starting every day with some quiet meditation on the life-after, I am ready to do my best and not worry about the outcome.*

- *Once I have done my very best in this life on the things I am working on, then I have no regrets, no matter what the outcome.*

- *In the course of the day if the need arises, I will seek opportunities for quiet reflection to put things back in the proper perspective.*

5. See Your Abilities and Accomplishments Anew

You have enhanced your awareness of your abilities and accomplishments to date in Appendix A while reflecting on this component and how you feel about it. The sub-components you reflected on included things like financial status, social status, emotional status, physiological status, etc.

The objective now is to take the inventory you have as a starting point and eliminate any feelings of guilt, shame, etc.; otherwise these negative feelings can get in the way of further development. The inadequacies need to be addressed using the process outlined in Appendix B. Let's take an example to make the point clear.

Henry Waller, a man in his late fifties, feels highly inadequate regarding his financial status. His thoughts are, "Look at my friends I grew up with. I worked harder, took more risks, took on more responsibilities, made much more, and then this stupid

'Dot Com' plunge of Wall Street took away my hard-earned capital. I am now way behind my peers and almost sixty years old. There is no way I will catch up."

On reflection and with the objective of getting engaged in the process of self-development, Henry Waller hopefully will make the following observations:

- *My analysis of my present status is correct and I cannot change the past. All I control now is how I react going forward.*

- *It is of no value comparing my financial status to my peers because it will only frustrate me. I need to use my present status and see what I can do to improve on it. It's a lot like the game of golf. Whenever I get envious of the tee shot that another player hits and I try to hit mine better than his, I end up playing his game. He has better skills in his game and I end up losing. In golf I need to focus on my last tee shot and try to improve on that. Maybe I should pursue a similar strategy here regarding my financial status.*

- *Some of the things I can do to improve my financial status from my present situation are the following:*

  - *Instead of retiring at age sixty-two as I was planning to I will commit to working until at least sixty-five and maybe a little longer.*

  - *We can cut back on the level of our lifestyle and achieve substantial savings.*

  - *We do not have to have an extravagant vacation every year. A simple vacation closer to home can be just as fun and relaxing.*

  - *I will talk to my wife to see if she feels like she can handle a part-time job for a couple of years to increase our revenues.*

  - *In fact, this plan to continue working might just be better for our health long-term than retiring and missing out on that feeling of accomplishment.*

What Henry Waller has done in this analysis of his financial status is to take what he perceived as a liability and turn it, almost, into an asset. He feels better about himself, his self-image improves, and his self-development moves forward.

For practice, here are some situations for you to work through. Imagine you are a friend and a confidante of the person in each of these situations. What advice would you give these individuals? Then you can work on your own abilities and accomplishments.

- *On reviewing his social status as part of his abilities and accomplishments, Timothy Cellar is embarrassed about the jail time on his record for armed robbery. Tim feels strongly, "Why bother? I will never get a fair shake in getting the kind of job I want. I will always be behind others and never catch up."*

- *While reflecting on her physiological status, Lorraine Dyer says to herself, "Why me? I have had more than my share of problems with that auto accident, cancer, and now the fall off the treadmill. It's not even worth it to try to keep myself in shape. I might as well just stay home and count down my time."*

6. Create a Potential That Does Not Limit You

What comments did you come up with regarding your perception about your potential? This is so very important for self-development. How you perceive your potential can either limit or expand your growth and development. Let me present two different perceptions of potential of a fifty-five-year-old individual:

- *I had my time to do new things when I was younger. Now is not the time to try new things.*

- *There is nothing I cannot do if I have the skills I need for the task. My being fifty-five years old has no bearing. What counts are my skills, my abilities, and my confidence.*

As you define your potential, here are some thoughts to generate a potential that is not limiting in nature:

- *Create high expectations for yourself. You have heard that children live up to or down to their expectations. The same is true for adults. Unfortunately for us, we cannot rely on others to generate high expectations for us. Hence, we should create our own high expectations.*
- *Think about your personal vision and consider what kind of potential you should define to reach your vision.*
- *At a minimum, your perception of your potential should include your role as a leader.*

7. Refine Your Perceptions of Others

Interactions are at the foundation of leadership, coaching, relationships, and more. One of the key components of interactions is what we believe about others: about people in general and about groups and individuals in particular. The outcome from our interactions is a function of what we believe about others, and how we react is a function of what we believe. If we do not go through a conscious and deliberate process of analyzing what is in our mindset about what we believe about others and address it, then by default the prejudices and biases that we grew up with will influence our interactions. And we are not aware of this influence, since the linkage of our beliefs to our behaviors is automatic. Hence the critical need for a process of reflection, analysis, and addressing our mindset.

As an example, a belief about people in general might be either of the two below or something in between the two. For each one of these beliefs, reflect on how it will influence the behaviors and interactions of the person holding it:

- *People will exploit you if they have an opportunity. People are not to be trusted. You need to watch your back at all times.*
- *I believe all people are like me. They are born wanting to do a good job and all people love a pat on the back when they do a good job.*

What belief would you want your manager to have? What believe would you want a person with whom you have a relationship to have? Now think about yourself: What belief about people in general would be appropriate for you?

Now reflect on your beliefs about groups of people and specific individuals in your personal and professional life. Think about the first one or two generalizations for each of these groups that comes to your mind. To enhance your self-awareness and maximize your self-development, try not to do any self-censorship. This is just for your awareness and not for sharing with others. To help you get started, here are some suggestions about groups you should reflect on:

- *people from other racial, ethnic, and cultural groups*
- *overweight and underweight people*
- *people who speak different languages and have varying accents*
- *people with physical and mental disabilities*
- *people with a different gender than yours*
- *elderly people, children, and teenagers*
- *people with a different sexual orientation than yours*
- *different functional groups where you work, such as human resources, finance, accounting, union workers, upper management, administration support, etc.*

What we believe about groups leads to stereotyping of individuals based on the groups they come from. Not only does this impact the person being stereotyped, it says something about us as to why we might stereotype. It could be a deficiency in our self-image that is causing the stereotyping. The deficiency in the self-image can make us feel inadequate. One way to compensate for this feeling of inadequacy is to stereotype others. By looking down on others, we elevate ourselves. While this might feel good in the short run, in the long run the deficiency re-surfaces to take a toll. Hence it is in our interest to rid ourselves of the tendency to stereotype others.

So, what would be a good program in our mindset regarding what we believe about others? A good starting point is to reflect on this: What would you want others to believe about the group you come from and about you specifically? Here is my suggestion of the kind of belief about others that will lead to positive interactions and productive outcomes from the interactions:

- *As human beings we are all alike in the sense that we have the same wants and desires and are driven by the same needs.*
- *Every group is like any other. Every group has its share of members who have achieved success and its share of members who have failed.*
- *Every individual is like me, wanting to do a good job if given the opportunity.*
- *The differences in achievement and effort seen in the workplace are the result of the environment, including socialization, upbringing, and opportunities in education.*

8. Hone Your Expectations of "Self" and "Others"

Any time we experience stress, two components determine the magnitude of the stress. One is the outcome from the situation and the other is our expectations. The outcome we cannot always control. Our expectations we can control one hundred percent. Hence it is critical to program expectations into our mindset that will be supportive of our growth and development.

Imagine a situation where manager Karl has high expectations of his employee Al. Karl does everything he has learned in the many training programs to provide Al with the support necessary so Al can do his best work. Three months after Al is hired, Karl is shocked to learn early one morning that Al has been arrested for a mugging. Karl is devastated that he trusted Al and had high expectations that didn't do any good.

The answer in this case is not that you should not have high expectations for those around you. The answer is that the high expectations need to be balanced with an awareness of real-world expectations. Hence, Karl should have had high expectations to help Al do his best work and simultaneously should have had real-world expectations that there was a lot about Al he did not know. This awareness would have prepared his mind for the kinds of disappointments and negative outcomes that can happen and would have cushioned the stress and frustration he felt.

Analyze the situations you are involved in at the present time and reflect on the people in your personal and professional life and create the two levels of expectations. In your consideration here are some factors you might want to include:
- *people you work with*
- *projects you are responsible for in the workplace*
- *things you are working on in your personal life such as going to school or involvement in a fitness program, golf league, etc.*
- *people in your personal life*

The Fun Is in the Journey

Now that you have gotten engaged in the process of self-development, you will find that it is a continuous life-long process. Using the analogy of golf, every small improvement in golf skills makes a golfer look forward to the next golf game. So also in the process of self-development, every incremental improvement in self-esteem drives re-engagement in the self-development process to take it even higher. Now it has become a self-motivating cycle, repeating itself forever.

While physical skills become limiting in golf – after all, there's a limit to just how far one can improve – this isn't the case in the process of self-development. So, enjoy the journey!

Index